Dear Son

what I wish I'd known at your age

by
Roy Sheppard

To Richard,

May be there's something of interest!

centre

First published in 2013 by
Centre Publishing,
Croft House, Clapton, Radstock, Bath
Somerset, BA3 4EB England.
Tel: 00 +44 (0) 1761 414541
Fax: 00 +44 (0) 1761 412615
Email: info@DearSonBook.com
Web: www.DearSonBook.com

A catalogue record of this book is available from the British
Library.

Paperback: ISBN 978-1901 534-214
Book cover design by Roy Sheppard.
Cover photograph © Peter Simonson 2012
Cover models: father and son Paul and James P Whatmore
Book design Antony Parselle

Dedication

To my dad for providing me
with such a powerful
moral compass

table of contents

introduction..page 5

what I wish I'd known about:
being a man...10
work..16
money..27
my emotions...38
 what you need to know about:
 self-esteem...45
 attitude...57
 happiness...60
 being a kind man...77
relationships with others...86
women...91
dangerous women...103
marriage and divorce..116
sex..127
decision-making...134
risk, responsibility and reputation.......................139
power..142
negotiating..144
life skills...151
random stuff...153

some final words..154
IF...156

introduction

Every man has, deep within him, a powerful force we can call 'man energy'.

Unfortunately, tens of millions of teenagers and young men (especially in the western world) are no longer taught how to use it properly. It's a bit like being equipped with a powerful V-8 engine but only knowing how to put your foot on the accelerator pedal. You may make a load of noise revving your engine but it won't actually get you anywhere. While enjoying the thrills of making all that noise, it's so tempting not to listen to anything parents have to say. If only you were able to hear them above that noise, you'd know that all they're trying to do is explain how to put that engine of yours into gear!

Your man energy is what will fuel your future life. This book of wisdom from about a hundred men with different life experiences is designed to help you gain a better understanding of the inner power you have right now and how it will continue to grow in the next few years. And provide you with practical guidance on how to put yourself 'into gear' so that you can go to some great places with your life.

Your man energy comprises a combination of physical strength, your drive and determination, humour, ambition, passion and a range of other intense (and at times, frighteningly intense) emotions.

The active ingredient that gives your man energy

its potency is testosterone. It's at the heart of what makes you a man. It would be easy to argue that testosterone is the single most dangerous natural chemical on this planet – responsible for so many pointless wars, millions of murders and shocking violence against other men, women and even children. If testosterone was in court on a charge of being an accessory to obscene levels of criminal, violent behaviour, it would get locked up.

However, in testosterone's defence, it has also provided every man who has ever lived with the 'fuel' to achieve true greatness in their lives. Your man energy has the potential to do exactly the same for you – but only when you fully understand it and apply it in helpful ways; to you and all those you eventually live, love and work with. Learning how to tame this beast inside you will make a massive difference to you in years to come.

Talk to any intelligent man and he'll admit (eventually) that his early life as a man was about pretending to be what he thought a man should do, think and look like. As for what he 'felt' at that time – he had absolutely **no** idea about his emotions! All he possibly knew was that he felt 'bad' much of the time, awkward, uncertain, confused, frustrated, horny, angry, resentful and misunderstood. And on top of that no one ever took him seriously. So he didn't take anybody else seriously. He was sick and tired of being told what to do by parents, teachers or anyone else who came into close proximity. And how do young men cope with it? We all put on a 'front'. We need to look as if we know what's going on. But we don't.

It takes men far more years than you can imagine

to get their head around what it is to be a real man. I was probably in my early forties before that happened. The majority of older men I know have told me very similar stories.

A critical part of being a teenage boy, is wanting to cut your mother's apron strings in order to be more independent. This coincides with a very real identity crisis for many mothers. They are now faced with two things. No matter what, they can't be a man and many become increasingly aware that teenage boys need male influences (especially single mothers who have devoted the past few years juggling their lives and making huge sacrifices to be a good mother). And secondly, they start to question who they will be once their child or children leave the 'nest'. In many cases, their identity is so wrapped up in their role as a mother, they may fear they will become completely redundant. They may fear the bond they have carefully nurtured with their son over so many years is about to be broken.

It *is* about to change, but it doesn't necessarily have to get broken as the son transitions into becoming a man. So some mothers (whether single or not) unknowingly or deliberately try to maintain their son's dependency on them by attempting to prolong their close involvement – for all the best reasons. But the more the mother tries to get closer to her son, the more he will feel compelled to pull away. And if the dad suggests the son be allowed to spread his wings a bit, the mother may then believe her feelings are being ignored or undermined. It can hurt everyone!

It might be helpful to think of parents as

'hands'. Some children grow up with both of these hands wrapped around them, sharing the role of supporting, nurturing, protecting, guiding, occasionally punishing and repeatedly dipping into their pockets to pay for everything. Sometimes the son only has one of those hands to provide for all his needs. And in other cases he grows up without any hands available to him at all.

Whoever may have handed this book to you cares deeply about your well-being and future happiness. They know that you are entering the next stage of your life as you transition from being a child into a young man. They know that you need to assert your independence and are prepared to step back to give you the space to do so. Your needs are being taken seriously (whether you are aware of it or not). However, you will encounter situations and experiences that are new to you. Stubbornly insisting that you need to do everything on your own is not always a sensible idea. Part of being a mature person is knowing when to ask for help.

In this way, I hope that this book will provide you with invaluable practical help, but also act like a bridge between parent and son. Ask anyone who knows how bridges are built and they will tell you that they are always built from both sides simultaneously. Refusing to collaborate with parents on the opposite shore will simply make it unnecessarily difficult for you to build that bridge on solid foundations.

Once that bridge has been established, with that V-8 engine of yours fully powered up and put into gear, you'll be able to drive far more confidently and skilfully into adulthood.

So dip in and out of this book. Some topics will

be more relevant to you than others. But that can change quickly. What you believe about something today could be very different to what you thought about the same thing only six months ago. Revisit topics. Discuss them with your friends and adults to arrive at your own opinions. Ask your parents about their lives before you were born, what they have learned about life, their fondest memories and the lessons they have learned.

what I wish I'd known about:

being a man

The blunt, down-to-earth British actor Sean Bean has played tough, gritty, 'real' men all his life; alpha male heroes and villains in movies such as *Lord of the Rings*, *Troy* and *Goldeneye*. As an actor he 'pretends' for a living. He's so good at it, that he's become rich and famous as a result. But in his 'real' life as a man he's a devoted dad to his daughters, he loves gardening and plays piano. Being 'tough' is not a prerequisite to any of that. Is he any less of a 'real man' than the characters he plays?

What is a real man anyway? And what is a man for? Ask women this question. Their answers are fascinating.

There was a time (and it wasn't too long ago) when real men were defined as honest, reliable, principled, hard-working, honourable, thoughtful, wise, physically tough and strong as well as sensitive. But nowadays in our popular culture, film criminals, gangsta rappers and thugs are often held up as examples of 'real' men: uncouth, unreliable, arrogant, dishonest, disrespectful (especially of women), aggressive, violent, distant (or totally absent) and uncaring. As a result, so many men are generally described and dismissed as jerks and losers.

In 'primitive' cultures, men are brought up by a network of fathers, uncles, male friends and older brothers, and are taught by example to have a healthy pride for who they become as men. It's a big deal. Yet, in our so-called more 'civilised' societies, boys are often brought up in predominantly female environments: fathers go out to work, leaving early and arriving home late; most teachers are now female, and divorced fathers are often forbidden by judges to have any meaningful contact with their sons or daughters. It sometimes seems that men are no longer required to be a part of bringing up any children. And if a man shows any interest in being a positive role model for boys, he's instantly viewed as a possible paedophile! How did **that** happen?

Becoming, and being, a man in the modern world is tough. Part of the problem for teenagers is not talking about it because if you did, you'd risk looking 'weak'. This creates confusion and a sense of isolation for a lot of young guys. When you feel like this, it is so easy to shut yourself away even further. Immersing yourself in a virtual online gaming world or visiting virtual nightclubs appears to be a 'fun' solution when it distracts you and dulls the emotional pain. Ultimately though, it doesn't work.

If feeling isolated describes you – you are not alone. Millions of others feel exactly the same way – they just don't talk about it. Most males cope with it in one particular way. Steve Biddulph nailed it perfectly in his book *Manhood* when he wrote, *"Most men don't have a life. Instead, we have just learned to pretend."*

We so often adopt the qualities we think we like from men who are pretending to be someone else in the roles they play on TV, in movies, or in sport or music. Our own fathers often feature, but in a lot of cases it's for the wrong reasons; they are who we don't want to become because they're never there, always too tired or are too busy for us to have quality time with them. For many dads this is because they have spent years wearing themselves out working so hard, as their way of demonstrating that they are taking their responsibilities as a husband and father seriously. And then to add insult to injury – they're dismissed by their teenage sons! It can be painful for dads.

So – do you want to be a 'real' man or a 'pretend' man? What's the difference? Does it actually matter?

The best example of a 'pretend' man is a bully. Bullies pretend to be tough. They are usually 'small' inside and do their best to appear 'big' on the outside. Bullies almost always have huge self-esteem issues hiding behind their pretend image. With a deep-rooted need to 'protect' themselves or look big by putting others down, they feel a constant need to 'prove' themselves. Real men on the other hand are never bullies. Real men don't need to prove they're a real man. They just are.

You've probably already lost count of the number of times you've been asked *"What do you want to be when you grow up?"* But have you ever been asked this far more important question *"**Who** do you want to be when you grow up?"* Think about it.

Who you eventually become can either be an accident or part of what you decide about yourself right now.

For example, do you want to be a failure, a criminal who ends up in prison, a drug addict, a homeless person or a drunk in later life? Probably not.

But it's amazing how many men and women turn out that way. In some tragic cases, they become all of those things.

One thing's for sure, it wasn't part of their plan. Or maybe they simply didn't have a plan at all. Perhaps they were 'too busy' at the time. Are you too busy to decide who you want to be? Or perhaps it seems too much effort? How people end up in bad situations can be incredibly complicated. Bad luck certainly plays a part, but, in its simplest form, how our lives turn out is about the sequence of small, seemingly unimportant decisions we all make (or avoid making) every day of our lives.

How you make decisions will have a major impact on your future life.

As a child, all our decisions tend to be made by our parents or carers. By the time you become a teenager, you're probably sick and tired of having every decision made for you. But because so many young people in 'civilised' societies aren't allowed to make many decisions, when you finally have to, you don't always know how to make them! Only when you start having to make most of your decisions as a man will you begin to realise that having others make them all for you is actually much easier! A major part of becoming a man is about how you make large and small decisions, and then about accepting the consequences.

In some societies it's very different. In the poorest areas of the world, the most valuable village assets are their animals. It's common for seven-year-old boys to be given the job of looking after them. Boys are taught from a young age to understand what it is to be responsible and to make important decisions. They grow up quicker.

In the 1960s, a group of young children became part of an experiment by the psychologist Walter Mischel at Stanford University in the USA. These four year olds were given a simple choice: they could have one or two marshmallows. They could have one immediately. Or if they were prepared to wait 20 minutes, they would be given two marshmallows. It was a small decision. Or was it?

About 14 years later, these same children were tracked down. The researchers made an amazing discovery. The kids who were able to wait for 20 minutes were happier, more successful and effective at school, and more confident socially.

Their ability to make the decision to delay gratification by controlling their impulsiveness made a huge difference in their early years. We'll take a closer look at how to make better decisions in a later chapter.

Do you think people who end up in jail or as addicts would have been one or two marshmallows kids? My guess is they would say, *"Give me ONE and NOW!!"*

Knowing how important it is to your longer-term happiness and success to be able to control your impulsiveness will have a significant effect on what sort of man you turn out to be.

One of the biggest problems in our consumer society is that we are all bombarded hour after hour, year after year by messages trying to persuade us to buy all sorts of stuff that promises to make us happy, fulfilled, to look cool, sexy etc. The list goes on and on. The marketing of many products is designed specifically to make us more impulsive. We are brainwashed into believing we can have everything **now**. And we are told all sorts of crap to persuade us to **not** delay our gratification!

One of the main differences between real and pretend men is that real men have a world-class ability to spot bullshit. Pretend men, on the other hand, are the ones who always dish it out – to others and to themselves!

So – who do you want to be? A real or a pretend man? The rest of this book is designed to help you make better decisions about becoming a well adjusted real man. Let's get real, right now!

what I wish I'd known about:

work

Elliott is 20. *"When I was 16, my dad kept telling me that I should get a Saturday job. I didn't want to listen. He'd introduced me to a guy who seemed to like me. He was the manager of a local computer shop. Eventually my dad persuaded me to go to my first job interview. I was rubbish. Looking back I had no idea. I wouldn't have given ME the job! But I got it anyway.*

"I helped customers with their problems, got things to work for them and sometimes mended stuff. It forced me to talk to people. I felt really awkward at first but pushed myself. It was a pain to have to get up every Saturday so early, but after a while I got used to it. Not only that, after about six months the manager called me into his office. I was petrified. He sat me down and offered me a pay rise! I hadn't even asked. He told me how impressed he'd been with the way I dealt with customers.

"He valued knowing that I always showed up for work on time. And he really appreciated it if there was a problem I knew I couldn't handle, I'd ask him for help. That job really helped me.

"Quite recently I had a three week work placement at a company as part of my college course. One day a guy my age had to 'shadow' me. Even though I tried to get him to ask me questions, he

didn't say a word. All he did was sit there using his hand to prop up his head on the desk. He was totally uninterested. He just didn't 'get it'. In that moment I realised how much I'd learned from my first job. I didn't want to believe it at the time but learning the discipline of working was the absolute best advice I could have had from my dad.

"*I have a lot to thank him for.*"

There is always work that needs to be done. And there are people who are prepared to pay good money for the right person to do that work. If you want to be that right person, this chapter will help you.

The unemployment rate among young people runs at up to 50% in some countries. It's very tough in the job market. Working for a university degree has come with a very high price: massive levels of tuition debt and the realisation that these new degrees may or may not be relevant to potential future employers.

Companies are just not hiring like they used to. So there are far fewer jobs available, especially starting positions. Stories of graduates applying for jobs and never even getting replies – never mind jobs – are now commonplace. And those who are lucky enough to get a job interview then get told that they are competing with hundreds of other applicants, many of whom are equally over-qualified for whatever jobs are available. It can be really tough and demoralising out there. There's very little chance that things will get easier any time soon.

Therefore, decide today that **you** are a business. It's your time, your knowledge, or your muscle power that customers and clients pay for, if you know how to sell yourself to them. Even if there seem to be no jobs, you can still find meaningful work. The next few pages will show you how. And in the process, will arm you with real skills that employers or clients are prepared to pay you for.

Janet is a highly experienced career counsellor. She shared these insights:

"I see many men in their early 20s. Mostly these young men did not achieve their GCSEs (British school certificates) and have been working in low skilled jobs: labouring, stocking shelves, gardening, odd job type of work. At the point when they come to see me they are bored and realise that they should have tried harder at school and at least passed GCSE at C grade in their Maths and English. With just those two subjects they can go into trade apprenticeships. Sadly, many people haven't even got these basic qualifications. Often this is because they've been sidetracked along the way (peer pressure, substance abuse, a lack of confidence, computer games, parties, girls) or they have found it too difficult because of a lack of support or encouragement to work through it.

"How to get a first job (any job) requires being flexible, creative and proactive. Being willing to try anything, to offer filling in at a moment's notice if someone goes sick, doing some voluntary work just to get a foot in the door, or offering to work unsocial hours (if it's legal for their age), is going to make them stand out from the hundreds of others who want the same job.

"It's so important to get used to a work mindset.

It can easily start in the home: taking responsibility for part of the running of the home at an early age, washing the family car, clearing up after a meal, mowing the lawn, teaching parents how to use their computer or tidying their own bedroom (that comment never seems to go down well!).

"These types of activity strengthen their ability to be responsible and reliable. It also gives them confidence that they can do something well and a feeling of being part of a team. And if they play their cards right they may get a bit of extra pocket money too.

"A lot of the university-educated young men I see also have similar issues. In addition, they do not have enough relevant work experience, no connections in their industry/profession and if they haven't worked throughout their studies they can often have a very unrealistic idea about the work environment. Unfortunately, many have had depression and other health problems that have affected their careers."

So, let's start with some thoughts on what too many people don't understand about the world of work. By understanding this stuff, you'll put yourself at an advantage.

Firstly, you must decide to be worth more to your employer than they are actually paying you. You don't just do what you think you need to do for the money you are being paid. You need to do far more. It's absolutely essential that you are perceived as someone who really cares about delivering as much value as possible to the person or organisation that you are working for. If you aren't prepared to develop this mindset, don't be surprised if employers or clients refuse to take you on, let you go, or look for someone to replace you the next time they need work done.

> *"Nobody cares how much you know, until they know how much you care."* Cavett Robert, founder National Speakers Association

Caring about what your client, customer or employer wants to achieve is incredibly important. And you need to take on at least some of the responsibility for helping them achieve the result they're looking for.

This mindset or attitude towards work is probably the most important thing for you to realise.

Don't fall into the trap of being told by colleagues with a bad attitude what you can get away with. Learning a bad attitude will cost you in the longer run.

Joe is in his 50s, but vividly remembers his start in the job market:

*"My first job was when I was about 15, helping out in a local shop on weekends. Fortunately the owner was a family friend, because he took the time to quickly put a stop to what could have become a permanent bad attitude. One of my jobs was to sweep and mop up the floor at the end of the day. I was usually tired by then, and lazily swept and swabbed. After a few days of this he stopped me, took the broom and, forcefully taking long sweeps, said, '**This** is how you sweep. With energy and purpose. Because if you can sweep with energy at the end of a hard day you can do*

*anything with energy, and any boss you ever have will notice it. Never just go through the motions of a job, no matter how menial. Really **do** it. There will be time to rest when you get home.'"*

The following can't be overstated: you must be reliable. Your job is to make your bosses' lives easier. They must be able to rely on you. If you're unreliable you can't possibly make their lives easier. Practise this behaviour with your family and friends to make it part of who you are. Your boss must feel that they can count on you.

In many situations you may be part of a bigger project that relies on each person doing the right thing, doing it accurately and doing it on time. Someone unreliable can cause all sorts of problems – which can be irritating or very costly for your employer. I remember when I used to do a lot of filming – the one thing that was drummed into me from day one was never ever be late because you were part of a very expensive team. And if you were late, the money being paid to everyone else was being wasted while there was a delay.

Don't think that a few minutes don't matter. They do matter. Just because it's not important to you, doesn't mean it's not important to an employer.

Being reliable costs nothing but it makes a huge difference in how you will be perceived and how professional you will be seen to be. And it's one of the most common criticisms I've heard from employers when they hire young people.

If you're new to the working world, making sure that you are professional and reliable is essential, if you want to be taken seriously.

Get this right and you will stand out in a very positive way. It doesn't matter how good you are if you're not there. It's as simple as that.

Maybe you're someone who likes to party. Great. I'm not suggesting you don't. However, if you show up for work looking bedraggled or being exhausted you cannot possibly do a good job. Your ability to concentrate will be affected. Your energy level will be lower than normal. Your employer is paying for you to function at 100%. If you're barely awake or hung over, you can't do that. You don't deserve to be paid in full if you're not delivering in full.

Here's something else you need to be aware of that will also help you to score massive points with a client or an employer: showing initiative. Doing what needs to be done, rather than only doing what you've been told to do.

This requires you to think about what you're doing – at all times. And thinking about the needs of your employer. Imagine what it's like to be your manager – what would they do, expect or want you to do if something unexpected happened?

It's amazing how many people behave like unthinking robots – completely dis-engaged or disinterested in what they're doing and why they're doing it. A lot of people simply don't use common sense. It's as if they left their brains at home. To look at situations from your employers' perspective is very highly valued – and will cause you to act in ways that will set you apart from the others . . . in a positive way.

job interviews

An employer has a need. They need help and are busy people who would not waste their time asking to see you if they thought you were not a possible candidate for the job. All you have to do is show them that in choosing you, they will have made the right choice.

To get the result you want, you must understand fully what they want and then tailor what you say, how you look and how you behave to match it completely. Interviews are like performing in a play – for both the interviewee and the interviewer. No professional actor would perform without preparation and rehearsal. An amateur certainly can't afford to go into such a situation without doing at least some preparation.

When you walk into the interview, the interviewer will genuinely want to feel that in meeting you, the right candidate has been found. Most interviewers want an easy life, so make it easy for them – gently take the lead. This does not mean rushing in as 'personality of the month'. Aim for quiet self-confidence. Look upbeat, stand up straight and be friendly. They want to see if you'll fit in with their other workers.

Tell yourself that you can help them. Even though you may feel nervous inside, it's highly unlikely that the interviewer will know this. Use the interviewer's name – if you did not catch it, ask again. You will appear more confident using his or her name, and he or she will like it. As a young person it will usually be appropriate for you to show the respect associated with using the interviewer's last name and title (Mr, Ms, Dr, etc), but some industries or organisations are less formal and may use first names. Follow the lead of the interviewer.

Maintain eye contact; don't look nervously at the floor. When asked to talk about yourself don't blurt everything out; keep it brief, upbeat and relevant. You'll almost certainly get asked, *"What are you interested in?"* You must have an answer for that question. And you must sound enthusiastic about what you tell them. Rehearse beforehand so you don't 'um' and 'er' too much.

As part of your preparation find out as much as possible about the company. This can be done from their website. Speak to a few people who work there about what they do. Learning a lot about what the company does, how it fits into its industry, and how well it is doing will help to indicate your interest and seriousness.

To make a good impression, you should use this information throughout the interview. But do not make the common mistake of blurting it all out at once. Use the knowledge to formulate lots of intelligent questions about the company. Have them on a piece of paper if necessary. Let the interviewer do most of the talking. This way you will succeed in a number of ways: you will appear interested and, the more you let him or her talk, the more interesting you will seem! You will also be turning a one-sided interview into a two-way conversation. This is a technique you can and should use in all your relationships. Even for low level positions you can make a good impression by asking questions reaching far beyond the immediate job position. Gently weave into the conversation some of the following questions. They could also be of use at the end of the interview, when you will often be asked if you have any further questions:

- What are the key challenges the company is facing at the moment?
- Why do you think that is? What or who is the cause of this?
- Who are the biggest competitors and how are they doing? (If you've already done your research, as you should have, you'll know the answer to this one. How does what you are told compare with what you found out?)
- How proud are you to work for this company? Why?
- What is the company doing to cut its costs?
- What is being done to grow the business?
- What new technology is being implemented throughout the industry?
- How much of this technology is being used by your company?
- How would you describe the management style or culture of the company?
- If you could change anything about the company, what would it be?

What you are trying to discover is how open, forward-thinking and realistic they are. Is the company thinking in the past or the future? By asking leading questions, you will also demonstrate how well informed you are. In some ways the answers you receive are unimportant.

During the interview, concentrate on issues relating to their needs rather than just your own.

They are looking for someone to fill their needs, not someone who just needs a job.

When you know that the interview is coming to an end, gently take control by asking if there is anything else the interviewer would like to know about you. If not, thank them for the opportunity to meet and ask when you can expect to hear from the company. Most people don't ever think to ask for the job! So finish with, *"I'd really like to have this job. I am sure I can be helpful and do a great job for you."*

If you still can't get a job, create your own by becoming self-employed.

You can download a free audio course *How to Earn* from www.DearSonBook.com/howtoearn. It will remain free for as long as our Internet web host doesn't charge us if a lot of downloads take place. So get in early!

what I wish I'd known about:

money

Six millionaires and multi-millionaires have contributed their philosophies about money and checked this chapter for accuracy. This is information about money that rich people know about, but poor people usually don't.

The biggest mistake you can make about money is taking advice from people who don't actually have much of it! Those people often go through their entire lives looking for the ways to 'get rich quick'. And fail.

Genuinely rich people on the other hand, tend to get rich SLOWLY! Their wealth is accumulated over a very long period. And, contrary to what you may think from seeing celebrities in the media, the vast majority of rich people do not live a lavish lifestyle. They are rich because they keep their money – they don't waste it on expensive 'toys'. They are particularly careful with money. That's precisely why they have so much of it.

You can't be a high spender and become a millionaire at the same time. Who is better off? A high earner who spends it all each year, or someone who earns less, but invests some of it wisely? It isn't the first person.

So, you could do what most people do and end up broke. Or you can quietly adopt the behaviours of those who know the secrets of becoming wealthy and financially secure. You have a choice.

The earlier you decide to copy what genuinely wealthy people do, the more you are likely to benefit in the long term.

Think of your future life as one of those colanders used to drain cooked vegetables. By the time you reach old age, it's highly likely that you will have earned a few million (pounds, dollars, euros or whatever) over the course of the years. All that money was poured into your colander. But the question is, how much of it will you manage to keep, and how much will flow directly through it, down the plughole?

We're all so obsessed by money but just the mention of it can induce a glazed expression of utter boredom on most people's faces. Therefore, before you lose interest (!), do the following now and for the rest of your life. The next couple of paragraphs may be the most important in this book. If you are serious about building a healthy financial future, consider this very seriously indeed. If you only adopt one idea from this book – make it this:

From today, save 15% of everything you ever earn for the rest of your life.

One multi-millionaire who read this said, *"I disagree. Make it 20%."* No matter how much or how little money you earn – set aside this money before you do anything with your pay cheque. In other words 'pay yourself first'. This is important. Don't fool yourself into believing that you'll be able to pay yourself last.

Human nature being what it is, you'll have spent it.

This 15–20% of everything you ever earn is **not** spending money. It must never be used to pay for day-to-day expenses or things like holidays. This 'capital' should only ever be invested to generate **more** money. Because you are young, you have something going for yourself that older men don't have, and that's **time**. Earlier we discussed how rich people get rich slowly. That's what you're looking to do. Money that you put away for 40 years will earn you far more than money put away for only 20. Or 10. The sooner you decide to adopt this 15–20% habit, the more likely you'll benefit longer term.

Capital is used to generate additional money. This income or interest is then added to the original capital. The increased capital is then capable of earning even more money, which is again added to the capital. This is the effect of compound interest. Compound interest, over a very long time, will help you become wealthy.

Experienced, smart investors use their capital to invest in a range of different ways. Some are very safe investments which generally deliver lower incomes, while other investments may be riskier. To compensate them for the risk they are taking, they hope to generate higher rates of return for their money. Because of the risks, they could lose their investment too. The combination of high and low risk investments is called their portfolio. A well-balanced portfolio will strike the best balance between the level of risk the investor is prepared to take with the income they receive from those investments. You can do this yourself if you are particularly knowledgeable or you can entrust the role to a professional adviser – who you have to choose very carefully indeed. They absolutely must be someone who is a) licensed and b) works for your best interests, not their own.

Genuinely rich people (as opposed to those who just want to appear rich) invest their capital in a variety of different ways to create various streams of income, which, when added together, allows them to live comfortably from that income.

They no longer have to work for a living. Their money now works for them instead. In contrast, most 'ordinary' people are only a few months' salary away from personal bankruptcy. Don't allow yourself to become one of those people.

By adopting this simple and profoundly effective financial habit from a young age, you will also learn financial self-discipline and responsibility. You will learn to use money to your advantage, rather than allowing yourself to be one of the hundreds of millions who hand over their hard-earned cash every week to make others even richer than they are already.

In our image-obsessed society, poor people tend to spend a high proportion of money they don't have (!) on stuff they hope will make them look wealthy and successful. When they do this over a long period, they practically guarantee they'll stay poor.

Therefore, the first thing to realise is that being financially successful throughout your future life is all about how much of your money you keep. It's absolutely not about how much you spend, or the over-priced designer labels you spend it on.

Decide from today to make it a lifelong priority to keep more of your money.

what you must know about debt

Poor people are either forced, or they allow themselves far too easily, to go into debt, and end up having to pay out a lot more in the longer term. Slavery may have been abolished hundreds of years ago in the West. But it's back. And it's spelt D.E.B.T. Debt really is a cruel form of slavery.

Each time you accept debt of any type, you are effectively allowing someone to tie a long, almost invisible fishing line to one of your testicles. The more you need that money, the shorter and tighter that fishing line is tied! The shortest and tightest fishing lines are owned by your government. They spell 'debt' as T.A.X. For that, you have no choice. We are all indebted to our governments. In return, they use this money in a variety of ways. First, they pay the interest on mind-boggling, eye-watering levels of debt they usually blame the previous government for!

What's left funds lots of essential and some non-essential public services, our schools and public hospitals, pays state pensions to men and women who have been making contributions for many decades, and, of course, provides the funding for a military to defend (and in some cases to do far more than just defend) your nation.

Once we have paid our taxes, we are then free to spend whatever we have left in any way we choose. Although that's not strictly true, as we'll discuss a bit later. Anyone who feels that they don't have enough money left over to enjoy their life at the level they think they deserve, will 'choose' or allow them-selves to spend now with someone else's money, and pay it back later. In other words, to go into debt.

When you go down Debt Road (probably in a car you've bought on credit), your life is under the control of those who own all the money you are borrowing. By the time tens of millions of men reach middle age they have accumulated masses of large and small debts and other financial commitments: bank loans, mortgages and loans for school/university fees for themselves and/or their children (or if they pay cash, it comes out of income that has already been taxed. Ouch). Each one of these financial commitments is another line tied to their balls. No wonder so many middle-aged men feel trapped and unhappy. And that's the time when most divorces also take place.

Banks and credit card companies will fall over themselves to lend you money. They are particularly eager to lend money to students. They really want you to be in debt to them – from the earliest possible age. And they have miles and miles of fishing line at the ready for tying to your sensitive parts!

Realise this, an 'offer' of credit (the opportunity to go into debt) – is actually a request that could end up costing you a lot of money for many years. Banks and credit societies are not charitable organisations: you will be paying a lot for the privilege of spending right now. The interest you pay will substantially increase the total you spend. It may feel painless because each monthly payment seems low, but over time it all adds up – to a lot.

Therefore, do not go into debt unless you absolutely have to. The secret is to never find yourself in a situation where you have to go into debt at all! Although in reality that's almost impossible.

At some point, one of the biggest debts people take on is a mortgage on their home. What most don't realise is that you buy one home, but by the time you've made all the repayments, you've paid so much in interest that you've actually paid for more than two homes! In fact a lot of mortgage companies allow you to pay back the debt for a lot longer; 25 years instead of say, 20 years. You're made to think that they're doing you a favour with lower monthly repayments. What they're less keen to tell you is how much more interest you end up pay during those extra five years. And most of that interest gets paid in the first few years, when you barely pay off any of the actual loan.

One more money myth is the idea that a mortgaged home is your asset. It isn't. It's the bank's asset, not yours. They just give you permission to live there while you repay your loan. If you ever find that you can't repay the mortgage, the bank will take the home from you – potentially with all the cash you put into it, leaving you with nothing! A mortgage in your name is one of the shortest and strongest fishing lines that can ever be tied inside your underpants!

Anyone who knows a lot about money will say there is such a thing as 'good' debt. That's outside the scope of this chapter. But even the experts make massive mistakes. The global economic meltdown in recent years is a brilliant example of how debt can bring down seemingly invincible financial institutions, even countries.

credit cards

The moment you're legally old enough to have a credit card, you'll receive invitations to have them. But if debt is so bad – should you get a credit card? Definitely yes. In fact, there is a strong case in favour of having two credit cards: one for work related expenses, the other for personal use. And if you ever lose one, you'll have a backup. But never more than that. Forget store cards and charge cards.

However, when you have credit cards, never use them for credit purposes. The money you borrow from credit card companies is very expensive indeed. Only use credit cards for convenience. Pay off the balance in full on each card every month. This can be done automatically. Set it up with your bank. Credit card companies know that millions of card holders forget to pay by the due date each month – so they make a fortune from interest they charge per day on the outstanding balances.

An additional benefit of having credit cards and paying them off in full each month is how it improves your credit rating. This may not seem important to you right now, but one day it will be. You will almost certainly need to arrange some kind of loan in the future. By building a track record of being a responsible card user, you'll increase the likelihood of being granted a loan as well as ensuring that your future credit rating doesn't suffer if you're refused!

In short, build up your capital. Reduce or eliminate debt. And do it all for a long time. Is this possible? Yes. But you need to know who and what is trying to stop you. And how they so cleverly persuade you to dip into your pocket for them – so often.

being a cash crop

Today everyone is bombarded with countless messages every day in an effort to persuade us to give in to temptation; to buy that chocolate bar, to spoil yourself with that new designer label or the latest 'must-have' piece of technology. The human species has never had to face this much persuasion before. It's all designed to stop you from delaying gratification. And if you can't afford it right now – no problem. You can pay quickly and easily using a credit card. Now you know why you have to give your credit card details only once to companies like Apple. We've been persuaded to give them a backstage pass to our bank account! You can now get as many apps and music tracks immediately without ever thinking that you have to pay for them. How cool is that? For them it really is! And very profitable. Not only that, each time you buy something you tell them just a little bit more about what you like. That information is worth potentially more to them than how much you spend with them.

In the 1920s, for the first time in human history, factory production in the United States outstripped real demand. The population had to be persuaded to buy more so those factories could operate at full capacity and make the most profit. Companies came to realise that genuinely happy people didn't feel the need to buy much 'stuff'. That's not good for business. So what began was the development of the dissatisfied consumer. During the 20th century, women were the primary target for advertisers. Are you feeling plain and frumpy? Buy our clothes. Look like a film star, buy our cosmetics. One cosmetics company described their products as 'hope in a jar'. Hiring behavioural psychologists, marketers have learned precisely how to make women feel insecure, unloved or unappreciated. Women are then far more likely and willing to buy whatever it is they have to sell. Any idea why shopping is now called retail therapy?

In the 21st century it's our turn as men to feel bad about ourselves. Drink our beer, smoke our cigarettes and you'll feel 'better'. Afraid you don't fit in? Buy the same clothes as the coolest kids – you can then be cool too. If persuading you to spend money involves making you feel bad or insecure – so be it.

There is a brilliant TV commercial for a brand of antiperspirant aimed at young men which illustrates this perfectly. A sequence of shots show attractive women in various ordinary settings – and the same reaction by cleverly selected types of men who are 'just like you': the moment they see the woman they instantly sweat profusely through their shirts, under their arms. Then an older 'father-figure' voice-over 'knowingly' asks, *"Do you suffer from premature perspiration?"* A very witty way to allude to a young man's sexual anxiety – premature ejaculation. This manufacturer has perfectly tapped into a deep fear held by so many men. Pay up, buy our product or you'll risk embarrassing yourself the next time you just see a gorgeous woman! No women in your life at the moment? Millions of young men all over the world are prepared to try anything. Who knows, it might work. There is an alternative of course – wash regularly. Deodorants are not designed to cover up rank body odour for guys who don't shower!

Using the most sophisticated behavioural research and software, men are now being targeted on an industrial scale to extract as much cash from us as possible. And they don't care if you go into debt to pay for what you can't afford. They'll even make additional profit from you by offering you a financial plan – with 'easy' repayments.

Every waking hour for the rest of your life, you will be bombarded with opportunities to spend small or large amounts of whatever you earn. It's no accident that 'convenience stores' as so widespread.

It has become way too easy not to think about what you spend your money on.

Therefore, for one month decide to write down every single thing you spend money on. Do it every day for a month. You will probably get a shock when you discover how you are persuaded to fritter money away without even realising it. A lot of that money could have easily been used to boost your capital account.

Your ability to delay gratification is incredibly important if you are serious about building up capital. If your 'will power' consistently overpowers your 'won't power', you'll never get rich!

Therefore it is worth learning to delay gratification. Every time you stop yourself from spending money unnecessarily, you reduce your chances of going into debt and simultaneously free up money to be added to your capital.

what I wish I'd known about:

my emotions

Imagine this: you meet a man with two perfectly functional thumbs. For some inexplicable reason he has grown up being told that its cool to never use those thumbs. So he fumbles everything he tries to pick up. That's how most men seem to go through life when it comes to our emotions. Many men are even proud of their lack of emotional understanding. It's somehow unmanly. Yet it's our emotions that drive most of our thoughts, which determine our behaviours and the results we achieve. Your emotions need to be understood if you want to have a good emotional grip on your future life.

Teenage boys and young men are at the peak of their physical fitness. Sexually you are at your most virile. Your sperm is at its most fertile and your sexual stamina is at its peak. Young women are at their most fertile at this time too.

Your body is run on muscle and hormones. There doesn't seem much room for understanding your emotions. And all those hormones flowing through your brain mean your emotions seem to change by the hour, or even by the minute, for no reason at all! But it is not an exaggeration to say that a deeper understanding of how you feel, and a recognition of the various emotional states you can fall into, are key to your future happiness.

It will help you foster the good states and identify the early warnings of the bad, allowing you to head them off. All of this will have a big impact on how you interact with others (including women, of course).

In the same way that certain foods lead inevitably to emissions of unwanted gas, do you find yourself feeding your mind with so many unhelpful thoughts that it's only a matter of time before there's an inevitable and unwanted reaction: namely an 'emotional fart'?

Have you had recurring unhelpful thoughts that ferment and stew inside, until one day they can't be contained any longer? You might have lost your temper over something seemingly insignificant. Perhaps you spoke harshly and later wished you could 'unsay' whatever you blurted out. But you can't.

Do you realise that genuinely happy, calm and relaxed people don't suffer from these 'emotional farts'? They don't sulk, scream, shout or have tantrums. They're not 'difficult' or demanding. They don't whine and complain. Why could that be?

Could it be that their emotional state is in complete harmony with their surroundings? They tend to be emotionally stable and are quietly confident that they can cope with whatever life throws at them. They view life as it is, rather than being obsessed with the way it 'should' be. People with this type of emotional balance are highly appealing to others. And whether or not you feel like this now, you can learn it.

Daniel Goleman in his groundbreaking book *Emotional Intelligence* wrote, *"People with well-developed emotional skills are also more likely to be content and effective in their lives, mastering the habits of mind that foster their own productivity; people who cannot marshal some control over their emotional life fight inner battles that sabotage their ability for focused work and clear thought."*

Unfortunately for most young men, understanding their emotions is often a huge challenge. All that testosterone definitely seems to get in the way!

But is it possible to adopt and absorb these emotional skills? Yes. Becoming more self-aware is the first step. Recognising the triggers that set you off is a valuable, long-lasting life skill. Learning how to deal with them is even more valuable. That is what this chapter is all about.

your emotional core

Our Physical Core is the collection of deep muscles in and around the trunk and pelvis. This Core provides inner physical strength, flexibility and stability, protecting us from injury. Strengthening the Physical Core is a key objective in Pilates and yoga.

Much the same way as your Physical Core protects and strengthens you physically, a strong Emotional Core protects your inner emotional strength. Emotions can be so uplifting, yet the same power and intensity can cause untold pain and anguish, attacking our hearts and souls like a cancer.

The Emotional Core components are:
- Self-Esteem,
- Attitude,
- Happiness, and
- Kindness, combined with Compassion.

When you improve your self-esteem, you feel more

at ease with yourself. By accepting yourself, you become less 'needy' of others. Moving from a low self-esteem to a healthy one, also improves self-confidence. When you start exhibiting a natural sense of quiet self-confidence, you become more appealing to those around you. And to yourself.

Once you've improved your attitude towards yourself, this improves the attitude toward those you live and work with. Other people will almost certainly respond to you more positively. This in turn contributes to your sense of well-being. It also reduces stress, making you a calmer and more relaxed individual. This further increases the likelihood that even more people will respond better to you.

Combining an improved attitude towards yourself and others, with an improved self-esteem, increases the likelihood you will start to feel happier in yourself. You can amplify this even further by adopting simple, yet effective happiness strategies, which again strengthen your entire Emotional Core. Each one feeds and nourishes the others. Of course all of this is much easier to say than to actually do. There are, however, a number of steps that you can take right now to improve your Emotional Core, which we will go into a little later in this chapter.

Talk to anyone who's had a personal tragedy, and they will tell you their lives changed forever in an instant. Accidents, illnesses and natural phenomena affect countless individuals every single day. Your Emotional Core is the best insurance to cope with the effects of personal traumas.

The benefits to you and to those who come into contact with you have the potential to be monumental and long lasting. The more you attract other people, the more you realise improvements you have made have a direct contribution to the way others view you.

explode

Of course, we all have faults and farts. Some minor, while others are far more serious and have a hugely damaging effect. An under-developed Emotional Core can be a trigger, turning minor faults into major ones.

We all have our own ways of coping with stress or being upset. Taking it out on those closest to you isn't going to make you more appealing to them. Or to anyone else. Screaming, shouting, and tantrums are common among young children, but take those behaviours into adulthood, and you'll find that it's simply not acceptable.

In violent family environments, it might be seen as 'normal'. It isn't. If you have such experiences, you need to unlearn some of those behaviours in adult life, if you are going to function as a more effective person.

implode

Have you learned to totally contain your emotions? Some people never show them. This isn't healthy either. It's often the case of children in families where parents don't express themselves openly and respectfully. Have you learned to deal with your own emotions by 'imploding'? This is a bit like a cartoon character that swallows a stick of dynamite. The dynamite goes off and the character blows up like a balloon before returning to its original shape. They open their mouth and a small whiff of smoke completes the comedic effect. The only problem with this 'solution' in real life is it never tackles the root cause of the suffering. And each time you get upset for any reason, the latest suffering gets added to your 'collection'.

The following provides another example of how someone with an under-developed Emotional Core might react to a situation lacking sufficient information.

In his book, *Don't Sweat The Small Stuff*, the late Richard Carlson PhD described unhelpful thoughts as 'snowball thinking'. A small snowball thought gathers more and more unhelpful snow, until it has grown to an enormous size. If you are spending a lot of time on your own, thinking about yourself, your life, what you feel you deserve but are not getting, opportunities missed, regrets and unfulfilled dreams and desires, it is fairly likely a small snowball thought will similarly gather size and importance. But only in your head.

An example of 'snowball thinking' might start along these lines. Someone has said or done something that you don't understand. Nothing 'bad' as such, but a bit confusing. So what do you do? You start thinking about it. In fact, you try to analyse it, over and over again. This tiny snowball is starting to gain in size. Because you have now devoted so much time thinking about it, you have finally figured out what it 'really' meant. What was originally a theory has now been allowed to become a significant issue. Now you have convinced yourself that you 'know' what it meant. And it wasn't good. In fact, it is now proof that yet again someone has disrespected you. Or they have failed to live up to your expectations.

How could they? What a bastard/bitch! Now, step back... What if the original thought wasn't triggered by someone else but from you? Blaming yourself can cause even more damage to yourself.

Either way, the other person is totally unaware of any wrong-doing. Why? Because there was no wrong-doing. But how do you think they'll get treated the next time they get together? This 'snowball thinking' will almost certainly lead to a massive 'Emotional Fart'!

Have you ever had any such experiences yourself? Either as a victim or as the perpetrator? Almost certainly. We all have.

But here's the critical point: the above reaction had nothing to do with the person's original behaviour. It was entirely down to the fact that your 'snowball thinking' attached a series of incorrect meanings and assumptions to that innocent behaviour. This is the problem with over-analysis. As each wrong assumption is added into the mix, its destructive power grows. What needs to be recognised is how and why those assumptions came about in the first place.

Our past relationship experiences create our life story. Unfortunately, in so many cases the story we tell ourselves is different from reality. When we combine all the wrong assumptions, judgements, interpretations, distortions and filters we end up with a mishmash of half-truths, confusion, suffering and insecurities. Most of which we are not even consciously aware of.

What recurring thoughts do you have that are not helping you lead a happier life?

Imagine your life if you didn't spend so much

time exhausting yourself by giving these unhelpful thoughts more attention than they deserve. It is possible, and doing so will make you a far more appealing person – to yourself and to others.

A well-developed Emotional Core protects you. It provides you with more emotional stability, flexibility and inner strength. When you know deep down you have a stronger Emotional Core, those resources help you cope with everything life throws at you.

what you need to know about:

self-esteem

How's your self-esteem and self-confidence right now? And how is it affecting the way you view yourself, how you interpret situations and the way people perceive you?

Self-esteem is the first of the four Emotional Core components. Let's explore what self-esteem is, how your past and current thinking patterns and behaviour influence your self-confidence. First the good news: weak, needy and inadequate 'victims' with little or no self-confidence and low self-esteem are in high demand these days.

Now the bad news: controlling bullies just love 'em.

And the more insecure and unloved anyone feels about themselves, the easier it is for the unscrupulous to entice them into a life of unrewarding servitude, keeping them under their control by dishing out daily doses of cruel put-downs, psychological and emotional, as well as physical abuse. And each time they get away with it, it confirms in the mind of the victim that they 'deserve' such harsh treatment because they really are that inadequate. In many cases, those with chronically poor self-confidence sentence themselves to years of emotional torment and abuse because they are willing to settle for anyone who shows interest in them.

On a scale of 0–10, how high is your self-esteem and self-confidence right now?

Extremely low self-esteem can mean you always feel deeply unhappy and sense that you get walked over all the time, but you're not quite sure why. So less than a 5 is a sign that you would benefit from giving your self-esteem some much needed attention.

Anything above a 5 is fairly healthy, although there's probably room for improvement. Is it possible to have self-esteem and self-confidence that's too high? Yes. Being 'egotesticle' (sic) will turn more people off you than will be attracted to you. Extreme selfishness or believing that the world revolves around you can make you deeply unappealing to others.

Aim for 'Goldilocks self-esteem': not too much, not too little, juuuuust right. Without a healthy self-esteem, emotional instability is practically guaranteed. That applies whether your self-esteem is too high, or too low.

reservoir of suffering
Each time someone calls us hurtful names, especially people who claim to love us (and even more so those we call ourselves!), the remarks flow into what I call our Reservoir of Suffering. At the bottom

of this reservoir is our self-esteem. It just sits there minding its own business. But as each new 'hurt' gets poured on top, that self-esteem is crushed by the sheer weight and pressure bearing down on it. Much like a shipwreck at the bottom of the ocean, our self-esteem is confined to the depths of our despair. Our self-esteem is drowned by the combined effect of these slurs and put-downs.

Low self-esteem directly affects the relationship you have with yourself as well as your relationship with others, your physical and mental health and your attitudes towards sex: turning some people off sex entirely or leading to a sex addiction in others. It can also lead to eating disorders as well as drug or alcohol abuse. Increased stress induces irritability, headaches and stomach aches, accompanied by a recurring sense of feeling overwhelmed. Constant tiredness and wanting to sleep or just to lie down during the day are all symptoms of stress. Sleep is an escape.

However, extended sleep among teenagers is not only about stress. Feeling velcroed to your mattress is actually quite natural. Your body is now growing at the fastest rate throughout your entire life. It is exhausting. And a lot more sleep is often necessary.

Low self-esteem can lead to a combination of other debilitating emotions and behaviours that make life even more miserable. But it can be improved if you decide to make it a personal priority. Let's see how, for the benefits can be life transforming.

Commercial divers lift precious artefacts from the depths of the sea to the surface by attaching buoyancy aids to help with the lifting. So it is with salvaging your own self-esteem, one of the most precious cargos you possess. It can take a while, and requires some effort on your part. Especially when you consider how many forces are at work to push it down again.

Propaganda experts know that the lies and distortions they spread become 'facts' if they get repeated enough. But you can make this same process work for the good, too. Repetition is the key to improving your self-esteem. This is why making daily affirmations can be so effective. The more time you choose to invest in improving your self-esteem, the quicker and easier it will be to make and see long-term improvements. You really can do it.

Help from friends will add even more oxygen to fuel your recovery and inflate those buoyancy bags to lift your self-esteem back to the surface. So, make a decision to adopt small improvements every day.

Men especially, perceive asking for help as a sign of weakness: proof that we are indeed as pathetic as we have been told. We have too many problems, not enough time, or not enough money to do this 'right now'. These are excuses, not reasons. Asking for help is not a weakness, but it can be a solution.

your inner critic

Sadly, after years of being put down, or being made to feel bad about yourself, we learn to put ourselves down before anyone else can 'get in first'. By doing this, we are fooled into believing we have insulated ourselves from being hurt by others, but it's the equivalent of punching ourselves in the face. Nip this in the bud by recognising when you do, then stop it!

Often we've faced years and years of insults and put-downs from a parent or so-called friends who, despite this, profess to love and care about you. If that's the case, whatever they say must be true, right? Wrong! However, our inner critic often agrees with these put-downs. Even though the basis for the put-downs is false, we often believe them.

We all have an 'inner voice'. This voice can be supportive or destructive. The inner voice of those with low self-esteem tends to become their most savage and vicious critic.

If you're thinking right now, *"I don't have an inner voice."* That was it!

Our inner voice can be encouraging, helpful and supportive. Yet all too often it's a savage inner critic. Think of this voice as a potential coach. If you were an international athlete, how well do you think you would perform if you were constantly told how incapable you were of winning any races, or improving on your previous 'personal best'? Who would want a coach like that? But it's surprising how many of us allow our inner voice to drag us down. Its motives are sometimes honourable. Unfortunately, it doesn't always do a great job. Well meaning it may be, but it can get a lot of things wrong about you.

For example, if your inner voice thinks you won't be able to achieve something, it may be negative in order to protect you from feeling so bad when (not if) you fail. The voice knows that if you don't try something, you cannot possibly succeed. Therefore, you don't try, you therefore fail to succeed and the voice proves that it was correct.

Whatever you do to rebuild your self-esteem, much of that effort will be wasted if you don't redefine the relationship you have with that inner voice. No matter what progress you make in other areas of your life, if your inner voice is highly critical, it will scupper most of your efforts, dragging your self-esteem back down to the bottom of your Reservoir of Suffering.

That voice has been with you for so long, you have probably never questioned the accuracy of anything it has said to you, or its motives. Your inner voice can be your own personal ambassador, but often it's an assassin.

What scripts has your inner voice used against you, perhaps for decades? Does it tell you what you aren't capable of? Why you don't deserve to be happy? How and why you are unworthy of anything better?

how to take back control

How might you behave differently if your critic was not trying so hard to control you? Remember this voice is not you. It's someone who wants to control you. Give your inner critic a name. It doesn't have to be a flattering one. You can disagree with this voice. You can argue with it. Although it's probably not a good idea to do this aloud unless you know you are alone! Confront your critic. Prove your critic wrong. Ask or even tell your critic to shut up. When you hear negative comments from your critic, yell at it *"Delete, delete, delete."* or *"Shut up and get lost." "You're poison. Go away."* Come up with your own comments if these aren't strong enough for you.

What if you could turn down the volume of your inner critic, or even switch it off? Actually, you own it, and can do with it whatever you want. Do what you want, not what it wants.

Let's suppose you have learned to believe you are stupid. You can prove such an idea is totally incorrect. Let's do it. For the purposes of this exercise, make a list of situations or incidents where you have behaved in a way that demonstrates conclusively that you are not stupid. What good decisions have you made? What good results have you created? What are your best achievements? At first, you may find it difficult to come up with examples, but despite negative comments from others and hearing your inner critic, you have achieved a great deal in life!

Universal put-downs that go unchallenged contribute to at least a dampening of an otherwise healthy self-esteem. When you hear your inner critic using words such as "always", "never", "you should", "you must" – challenge it; demand proof that what it says is true. When you become more self-aware, you may discover these words are used far too much. In fact, remove the words "should" and "must" from your vocabulary. These are 'loaded' words and easily lead to feelings of shame, guilt and disapproval. Become more aware of others who accuse you of "You always..." and "You never...". They are trying to exert power over you. Don't let them. Increased awareness will help you question the motives of those around you. In the same way critics have repeatedly put you down over the years, it's essential you learn a new habit of repeating healthy thoughts.

You might think this is silly, but it really works. Notice more of your successes. Every time you do something right, quietly congratulate yourself. You're slowly starting to prove your inner critic wrong, and clearing space in your mind for a constructive coach to contribute to your long-term well-being. This will help you become even more appealing to others.

practical ways to boost self-esteem

When you improve your self-esteem, you increase your options. You feel better about doing so, which in turn takes your self-esteem up a notch.

From now on, make a decision not to allow your inner critic to say anything that undermines you. Ever. And stop letting your inner critic blame you for anything. It's probably wrong about you – yet again! It may take some time to retrain yourself and silence your inner critic, but you can do it.

If others tend to put you down, decide to be more assertive with them, too. Being assertive is about respecting yourself as much as respecting others. Aggressive behaviour is not to be confused with assertiveness. Aggressiveness is the equivalent of marching into somebody else's country. Assertiveness is standing your ground to ensure nobody marches into yours.

Learn to say *"no"* more often. Wean yourself off the notion to say *"yes"* if you prefer to say *"no"*. The fear of disapproval often stops us. In reality, most people tend to think better of those with clear boundaries and who will not allow themselves to be taken advantage of. Someone who expects you always to say *"yes"* may be unhappy when you say *"no"*, but over the long term you may earn more of their respect.

If someone puts you down, or makes jokes at your expense, politely say, *"Please stop doing that. I don't like it."* If they dismiss your request, repeat what you said calmly and politely. Or you could respond by saying something like, *"Some need to put down others to feel better about themselves. I hope you're feeling a bit better now. Pick on someone else next time."* If they insist on making fun of you for being *"so sensitive"*, respond by saying that perhaps they are the one who's being insensitive! Or simply leave the room if you can. Just because you allowed this in the past, it doesn't mean it should be allowed to continue. It is better that they think you have no sense of humour than to allow them to make you feel bad about yourself. Just stop everybody from getting away with it. Do it calmly. There is no need to get irate or emotional about it. But learn to do it.

In general, stop letting others have what they want at your expense. Each time you allow this to happen, it chips away a little more of your self-esteem and reinforces any feelings of inferiority you might have. Stop making assumptions about what people think of you. You cannot read their minds, so don't be so sure they think poorly of you.

Identify the toxic people in your life: those who make you feel bad, deflated or worn out. Make a decision to minimise the time spent with them. If you can't avoid at least some contact, make a concerted effort not to tell them about your plans and aspirations so they won't try to talk you out of pursuing what you want.

Instead, invest more time with the people that make you feel good about yourself.

Who do you perceive as the authority figures in your life? Inevitably, parents are on the list. Gaining approval from these authority figures is usually important for most people, but there are some who are cruel and not supportive. If some of your authority figures have practically made a career out of putting you down, perhaps it's time to delete them from your list of people from whom you seek approval. After all, they've never done it before, so it's unlikely they ever will.

List everything you like about yourself. Ask your friends what they think you're particularly good at. Ask only those you trust. Don't include those who have been responsible for putting you down.

List your achievements. If it helps, carry a note pad around with you for a while, to write down your past achievements as you think of them.

Here are some other things for you to think about: What is working in your life? What isn't working as well as you might like? What actions can you take to improve the areas that aren't working?

Decide to do something new every day. Added together, little things can lead to big improvements. List all the places you want to visit and everything you've always wanted to do. From this constantly evolving list, find something each day to look forward to. Use your list to set yourself a new, personal 'enjoyment' goal every month: that's 12 new goals in a year. To make this happen, plan ahead more. Make appointments with yourself. And don't cancel on yourself. Your needs are at least as important as anyone else's.

Ask yourself questions like these:

- If success at anything was guaranteed, what would I do?
- What new skills could I acquire?
- What new hobby could I immerse myself in?

New activities can help you break out of the self-destructive thinking that leads to harmful introspection. Worry and guilt have been described as the 'pointless emotions'.

There are some extremely high-performing individuals in the world. Invariably they are incredibly busy, yet they look after their physical well-being by investing time in themselves for exercise and relaxation. You can do the same, but only after you decide to make 'you' a priority.

Invest time in making friends with yourself. Even though you may not feel like it, find ways to interact with other people.

When someone gives you a compliment, have the grace to accept it. From now on, never invalidate a compliment by dismissing what they have said. It is disrespectful of the giver of the compliment. Simply say, *"Thank you. That was a nice thing to say. I appreciate it."* Never say, *"Oh, it was nothing."* What you have done is not 'nothing'. Be more aware of what you allow into your head.

Accept that you can change if you want to do so enough. All change can be uncomfortable or even frightening at first. Acting 'as if' you have confidence in whatever you do can be a major contributor towards actually being more confident.

By making small changes and improvements, as

your confidence grows you become more inclined to make even more changes and improvements. Slowly you will start to notice a change for the better in the way you feel about yourself. Sometimes we can't seem to help what we think about. Especially if or when we are in emotional pain. You may not realise this, but you can change your emotions. All it requires is making a choice. You can decide to feel something more empowering and more useful to you.

To illustrate this, do the following exercise. Sit or stand. Look down at the floor; make your shoulders rounded and take on the appearance of a depressed person. Now, without changing your physical posture, try to feel happy. You will probably find this difficult to achieve. Next, stand up straight; look up; breathe deeply. Then, again without changing your posture, try to feel depressed. It's difficult to do so. One of the simplest and most powerful ways to improve the way we feel is to simply stand up straight.

We become what we think about the most. So, practise visualisation. See yourself being more confident and handling situations better. See those around you with happy smiling faces. Expect to be successful. This will improve the likelihood that you will follow through on your new behaviours. Experience feelings of quiet confidence and happiness. Practise your new behaviour with people who don't know you.

By adopting these behaviours, you can only become a more attractive person: to yourself, to those you know already and to everyone you have yet to meet. Attractiveness is not the same as being beautiful or handsome. Those are genetic qualities. Attractiveness is an attitudinal quality that arises from healthy self-esteem and an appealing attitude to life. Everyone can be an attractive person.

Learn to accept that it is OK just to be you. Become the person you are meant to be.

what you need to know about:

attitude

Attitude is the second pillar of your Emotional Core.

Spotting a bad attitude is so easy, isn't it? Unfortunately, it's far more difficult to recognise a bad one if it's your own.

All too often a lack of self-confidence and low self-esteem will manifest itself in a poor or unhealthy attitude. This in turn will often create more feelings of low self-esteem and even less self-confidence, leading to a worse attitude. It's a circle of thinking, believing and behaviour that can ultimately poison you.

Your attitude is one of the first things other people always notice about you. A can-do attitude is your most valuable asset. It's free. And it's worth looking after. It's been said that *"thought, attitude, behaviour and result"* is an ever-increasing circle or outward spiral of impact. By improving what you think, you change your beliefs. Change your beliefs and you change your behaviour. Change your behaviour and you change the results in your life.

The price of a bad or unhealthy attitude can be

huge. Not only to everyone else who comes into contact with you, but to you personally. A friend of mine told me this story. A particular guy always goes to see his son play football. Because he only ever talks about why his ex-wife was so horrible, the other dads wait to see which side of the pitch he goes to: they then go to the opposite one. When you allow your attitude to control you, rather than you controlling it, you become someone who is constantly reacting to your own emotions and moods and nothing else. In extreme cases, people will avoid you like the divorced dad just mentioned.

For many, it has taken years of diligent effort to achieve world-class status as a negative thinker. If you can identify with this, cleansing yourself of negative thoughts is likely to take a while. Accept that it will. Before any improvements can take place, you have to start with the simple decision that having a positive attitude is worth having and worth working towards.

This next exercise will almost certainly offer you invaluable insights. Take your time interviewing yourself (or do it with a trusted friend) using these questions and add any others you can come up with:

- What is your attitude right now? Why?
- How much does your attitude help or hinder you at the moment?
- How much are you a by-product of your moods, or is your mood what you decide it's going to be?
- What do you tend to do or say that might lead others to think that you have an unhealthy attitude at the moment?

- Who affects you positively?
- Who affects you negatively?
- Who do you spend time with who drain you?
- How committed are you to improving your attitude?
- What would you want people to say about you behind your back?
- What do you need to do differently so they would?

Let's be realistic here, very few people indeed are totally positive or totally negative all of the time. So learn to focus more of your attention on those with great attitudes. Who are the people you know who have one? I'd be prepared to bet that they attract other people like a magnet. They radiate optimism, energy, enthusiasm and vitality. Optimists tend to be happier, more successful and healthier individuals than those with negative attitudes. Spend more time with optimists. And make sure you are someone they would choose to spend time with.

Your attitude is linked to your energy level. You can quickly improve your attitude by increasing your energy. Enthusiasm increases energy. So learn to be more enthusiastic. Feeling tired? Ignore those feelings and just work through them. With some practice, you can nearly always work through it. Focus your attention on what's good about a situation and not what's wrong. Look forward to more things.

People with a great attitude are not 'Me Merchants' or 'I Specialists'. These are people who constantly talk about themselves. Some do so because they are intensely arrogant and self-focused.

However, others do it because they are incredibly shy and self-conscious, paradoxical as that may seem. They believe they have a duty to keep a conversation flowing. And because they don't know what else to talk about, they stick with a topic they know intimately well. Themselves!

Either way, people who talk incessantly about themselves are far less appealing than those who don't.

Dear Son

Talk less about yourself. Listen more to others. People will think you're great!

what you need to know about:
happiness

To gain a better understanding of genuine happiness, let's first look at unhappiness.

Happy people are often targeted by very unhappy people who believe they can suck happiness out of those who have it. And when it doesn't work (as it won't), things often get ugly for the victim who then also gets blamed for 'failing' to please.

Knowing more about the various facets of unhappiness, yours and that of others, will give you many insights into how you experience the world. And the effect you have on others. The nature of this topic might seem a bit 'down'; please ignore those feelings. This discussion is designed to help you.

what unhappy people do

I'm reminded of a chat I had with a young guy who claimed he wanted to be in a serious relationship. I started to ask him about happiness. A big mistake. He almost spat, *"I hate all that happy clappy crap."* I suspect if I'd been a woman he was interested in, he'd have hidden that. Maybe. But it would have come out sometime. Being that unhappy won't help his chances. When someone's default setting is 'unhappy' it will sabotage any present and future relationship.

"You complete me." was a great line from the movie *Jerry Maguire*, but think about the idea behind it just for a moment. If someone else 'completes' you, it actually implies you were imperfect, lacking and incomplete in the first place.

When you have a healthy self-esteem and an appealing attitude you are already complete.

If you are happy, do not get trapped in a friendship or relationship with an unhappy person.

Dear Son
Avoid unhappy people.

Do not start or allow yourself to get sucked into a relationship with an unhappy person. They will want or even insist that they be showered with attention. In almost every case, the giver (you) will fail to give 'enough'.

Therefore, it is essential you learn to identify unhappy people accurately and quickly before you get saddled with the responsibility for 'curing' someone of their unhappiness. It's a lesson in futility. It can't be done. Here are some of the telltale signs:

- Oblivious to the feelings of others, they are only interested in themselves, their own thoughts and feelings.
- They have more rules than they know what to do with. And insist on imposing them on others.
- Constantly finding fault with everyone except themselves, they seek and demand perfection.
- They actively seek conflict to justify releasing suppressed anger or rage.
- They are always *"so busy"*, either to impress others with their own sense of importance or as a strategy to stop thinking about what isn't working in their life.
- They attempt to control the uncontrollable and demand certainty for everything.
- They feel the world is against them. And things are harder than they need to be. They constantly play the role of a martyr.
- They are chronically fatigued, or want people to think they are, in order to reinforce their martyr status.
- Money is a prime focus, although they often squander it whilst complaining that they never have enough.
- They keep moving the goalposts. Nothing you do for them is right. Even when you do what they tell you, it is never enough.
- If already in a relationship, they aren't interested in the well-being of their partner and don't care about his or her happiness, success, aspirations or comfort. It's always *"me, me, me"*.

These are just some of the ways an unhappy person behaves. Much of it is linked directly to low self-esteem. They figure, either consciously or unconsciously, that if they can force people into giving them more attention, it gives them power and will satisfy their self-esteem needs. It doesn't. In fact, it often feeds an unappealing attitude which drives high-calibre people away. The only ones willing to put up with this kind of behaviour are others with low self-esteem, who are prepared to accept this level of unreasonableness. To them, any relationship at all is better than no relationship. Do not fall into this trap.

Did you read through the list above and recognise elements of yourself? If so, there is hope. You can benefit from applying many of the ideas you will find here. Adopting even some of these ideas will lead to many of these behaviours melting away. You can become happier. One of the ways is to realise that happy people don't make demands on others, nor on themselves. They accept things as they are, and find the courage to take action when improvements are necessary.

assess your current happiness level

- How much do you want others to be happy? Shrugging your shoulders and not really caring is a good sign that you're not happy yourself.
- What proportion of your thinking is devoted to what is wrong with your life?
- What proportion is devoted to what is good or even fantastic about your life?
- Does item 2 above get more attention than item 3?

On a scale of 0–10 how happy would you say you are 'most of the time'?

0 1 2 3 4 5 6 7 8 9 10

Where you place yourself on this scale is what psychologist Martin Seligman of the University of Pennsylvania describes as your 'set-point'. This set-point usually, but not always, remains fairly static through life. Generally speaking, whatever your set-point is today, it will be similar in 20 years time, too. That is, if you carry on with your life as it is today. This is key. Make a permanent change in your attitude towards life and you make a permanent change to your set-point as well.

Anecdotally, I have asked many people of different ages where they would place their happiness level on this scale. The younger people I've asked seem to have an average set-point of 6–7, while older men and women in long-term happy marriages seem to have set-points of 8+. In many cases, people tell me that they had never really thought about how happy they were, even though most of us want to be happy. Knowing your happiness set-point can be useful, even if it reminds you that you're basically quite a happy person. If you're set-point is quite low, you can improve it if you decide to make a conscious effort to do so.

Having used these ideas in my own life, my set-point is now about 8 most of the time. Ten years ago it was quite a lot lower, in large part because of my unhelpful thinking patterns. It really can be improved. Like everyone else, my set-point fluctuates downwards and upwards on occasion. Ecstasy and joy sometimes visit, too.

For me, I'll experience a 10 simply sitting on the pebbles looking out to sea from Newgale beach in Pembrokeshire, west Wales, near where I grew up. Watching the summer sun go down over St David's Head is only marginally better than sitting in the same place during a raging storm in the middle of winter. It always reconnects me with life. No matter where I am in the world, I've learned to mentally transport myself to that place whenever I'm feeling a bit 'down' or overwhelmed.

You may also have such a place that makes you feel good. Call up such special places in your own mind to help improve your mood when you are down. Visualising like this is a form of 'resourcing', storing pools of positive feelings and retrieving them when you need them.

However, we get so sucked into coping with the day-to-day, we often forget to do what makes us feel happy inside and what is most important to us.

If you are unhappy about elements of your life right now, you are not alone, even though you may often think you are. In recent decades, general levels of happiness in developed countries have dropped noticeably. Unhappiness has therefore become far more widespread. And the number of people suffering from depression has soared. According to the World Health Organization more than 120 million people suffer from depression, which is of course an extreme form of unhappiness.

Depressed people find it particularly difficult to be kind or loving, either to themselves or others.

mindset and match

Genuinely happy people think and behave in fundamentally different ways to those who are unhappy. There are countless people in dire poverty, enduring appalling living standards and some with horrendous physical handicaps who are far happier than those who appear (on the outside at least) to have everything they could possibly want from life. The way we think is the key.

A dear friend once told me how he often felt disappointed with himself and unhappy that he hadn't worked hard enough to achieve massive career success. He added that he hadn't really been that successful. I said, *"The next time you find yourself thinking in this way, take a very long, slow look at your son and daughter. Then ask yourself how successful you've been."*

He was stunned into silence for a moment. What followed was an overwhelming feeling of love for his children. As a truly devoted father, he'd allowed himself to forget about how much joy and happiness existed in his life already.

This is just one poignant example of how we all at times think ourselves 'down'. Unhappy people tend to be brilliant at this. Happy people recognise when they start to think like this, and have strategies that replace unhelpful thoughts with more empowering ones. They usually do this without even realising it. It is second nature to them. It can become second nature to you, too.

Happy people tend to remember to be happy. They fully appreciate what they have already. Unhappy people simply don't do that, they don't see any good in what they have, and they forget what being happy is. It's a learned behaviour. Ongoing feelings of unhappiness can be unlearned.

Invariably, unhappy people allow their unhelpful thinking patterns to focus repeatedly on what's wrong with their life. What's wrong with their body. They're too fat, too skinny, too tall, too short. Their nose is too pointed. Their penis is too small. Their fault lists are often very long indeed.

It's as if they're going through life constantly chopping and changing their activities in much the same way as they would zap from TV channel to TV channel, vainly trying to find something interesting to watch. And even if they find something, they still keep zapping channels just in case something better crops up elsewhere. That is how they go through life: always on the lookout for something better. They don't know exactly what they want, just something 'better'.

The mistake they make is never questioning the real reasons for their unhappiness, which is the first step towards unlearning it. The true underlying cause of unhappiness is often related to the amount of time they allow themselves to think about what's wrong. They take their negative thoughts far too seriously. It never occurs to them that by thinking so much about what they've put on their fault lists they guarantee they will feel worse about themselves. Concentrating on what is bad never makes you feel better.

- How often do you allow yourself to think unhelpful thoughts that deprive you of feeling happier right now?
- What are the most unhelpful thoughts you

tend to repeat to yourself regularly? Write them down.

In so many cases, the root cause of a person's unhappiness is because reality refuses to conform to the carefully constructed fantasy that has been allowed to grow inside their mind. They keep feeding it with notions of the way things should be in their life. In many cases, their fantasy becomes their reality. And the deep unhappiness which pervades their entire life is in the gap between the real world and how they feel it should be.

This is a critically important point. Everybody does it at times. But unhappy people tend to allow it to dominate their thinking. And unhappy people are likely to withdraw from other people, spending a lot of time on their own, so they do a lot of this type of thinking. When you drill down a bit deeper into why men and women are so unhappy, it's often their habit of over-analysing situations, coupled with a desperate desire to somehow fit reality to the fantasy they've created in their mind. It keeps them unhappy.

You can devote the rest of your life to complaining about what your life should be. Or you can make a simple decision to make the most of what it is on a day-by-day basis right now.

Dear Son
Your life is what it is. It is not the 'better' version you have created in your head.

Crucially, accepting this simple truth can have a massive and positive effect on your attitudes and behaviour towards other people. You are you. They are who they are. Trying to turn anyone else into your fantasy of what you have convinced yourself a partner or friend should be will not only lead to huge disappointment (and the resentment that accompanies it), but it can make the other person's life unbearably, and unnecessarily difficult.

Remember to accept your reality every day.

When you learn to remind yourself daily that your life just is, over time you will learn to accept it as being OK. Some days it will be less OK and on other days it will be a lot better than just OK.

deciding to be happy

Just suppose you could guarantee that you could change from being an unhappy person to a genuinely happy person in just eight hours. If it was guaranteed, how would you spend that time? Would you think about your problems even more? Or would you concentrate on adopting strategies that made you feel better straight away? Effective people devote a higher proportion of their available time focusing on solutions, not their problems.

In his work as a stress counsellor, best-selling author Richard Carlson PhD 'cured' countless unhappy people quickly, simply by helping them to adopt new thinking strategies. He often told his patients, *"Being upset by your own thoughts is similar to writing yourself a nasty letter – and then being offended by that letter."*

How many people do you know who effectively do that every day of their lives?

It all starts with making a decision to be happy. This then becomes a priority in your life. You give it your attention every day. Carlson explained to his patients that how each of us feels, right now, in this moment, is a direct result of what we are thinking right now. Your thoughts create your emotions. They are linked directly. Unhappiness is an emotion, triggered by unhelpful thoughts. Without those thoughts, you cannot feel unhappy. Unhappiness simply cannot exist.

Thoughts are not real. They are part of your imagination. He compared dreaming to the thoughts we have while we're awake. We know our dreams are not real, but we seem to want to believe that our thoughts while we're awake deserve to be taken more seriously. They don't. Just because you thought them, doesn't mean they are accurate or correct.

Unhelpful thoughts repeated over a long period have a devastating effect on anyone's well-being. And it's totally exhausting. So many suffer from perpetual self-critical patterns of thinking. These evoke deep and often painful emotions which trigger stomach-churning reactions. In many cases, creating a vicious emotional circle of pain and suffering. What we are unhappy about becomes what we think about the most.

Robert Holden PhD describes negative emotions such as guilt and anger as guests who often visit even though they have not been invited to come and stay. The same thoughts go round and round in your head, never getting resolved. Learn to recognise when unhelpful thoughts visit you, and invite them to leave. Mentally say, *"Oh, so it's you again. Please leave. I don't have time for you today."*

meet the 'hyper-happys'

On the other hand, pretending to be happy all the time won't make you happy. In fact, it could prolong your unhappiness. That's precisely what particularly unhappy people do.

Genuinely happy people are appealing to others. Unhappy people are less so. Far less so. Extremely unhappy people know this and will often go to extraordinary lengths to fool themselves and others into believing they are happy. And in many cases it's because they so desperately want to appear appealing to others.

These really unhappy people can be spotted quite easily when you know what to look for. I call them 'Hyper-Happy'. They have perfected the illusion of looking and behaving in ways that they believe represent happiness. It's usually too much. They are too 'up'. Too often. They don't seem to have down days. They are always wearing their 'happy face', and nothing but.

Party animals are an extreme example of the 'Hyper-Happy' type. Their obsessive, frenetic pursuit of pleasure, fuelled by large quantities of alcohol, recreational drugs, risky adrenaline-producing activities, and a one-night stand mentality, are in most cases a 'front' for deep unhappiness and inner turmoil. You will never meet a happy alcoholic who's still drinking, or a happy drug user. But they can be so good at making you believe they are. They are hedonistic stimulation junkies. 'More' is never enough. Even so, they always focus on wanting 'more' now. Surely that would make them happy? More of the latest designer clothes, a better job, more money, more expensive holidays, a newer car; then they would be happy. But it doesn't work.

Think about it: truly happy people really don't need to get 'high' when they are high on life already.

Yet, to the uninitiated, Hyper-Happys can appear exciting, dangerous and intoxicatingly appealing. And anyone who's not as happy as they'd like to be is often attracted to these types in the mistaken belief that some of this exciting happiness will rub off on them. It doesn't. Hyper-Happys are so self-obsessed they constantly feed off others, who inevitably end up getting used, abused and discarded. Alternatively, once the Hyper-Happy has you hooked, they drop the pretence, reverting to their real behaviour: namely being unhappy. They were happy when they met you, but now they're not, so it must be your fault. And that blame is often sufficient justification to make their target's life a misery. They effectively say, *"I am not happy, you haven't made me happy. Therefore, it is your fault I am not happy. And you are going to pay. I will then be happy."* It is flawed logic, but it's the best they've been able to figure out. After all, nothing else has worked.

These unhappy Hyper-Happys are convinced that somebody else and 'better' circumstances will miraculously transform them into being happy, 'someday.' The trouble is the 'somebody else' always fails, the 'better circumstances' don't seem to arise (nor do they make any effort to improve their circumstances), and 'someday' never comes. It's more of a happiness mirage: always somewhere in the distance, out there on the horizon.

Truly happy people on the other hand, may look really boring by comparison. At least at first glance. Their happiness is inside. And it doesn't always show in the ways described above. But it is visible in their everyday lives.

happiness heartbeat and habits

We all have what I call a 'happiness heartbeat'. It's an 'upbeat' for happy types and a 'downbeat' for unhappy people.

During periods of great joy, the happiness heartbeat of happy folk may beat more quickly. At other times, a deep, calm contentment permeates throughout their entire body. They are at peace with life. The heartbeat is slow and regular . . . and still upbeat. It doesn't need feeding by external factors. In fact, genuinely happy people don't need loads of 'stuff' to make them happy. They are happy already. Because they understand what 'enough' means to them, they don't bother consuming or buying the latest fashions or unnecessary faddish toys. Able to delay gratification, they also benefit from the added advantage of enjoying everything twice: once while looking forward to it (which costs nothing), and again from the actual experience.

Happy people are open to new experiences, new ideas and new people. How open are you to anything new? If not, why not? What if you decided to stop deciding why things are not a good idea? Say *"yes"* to more opportunities, just for the hell of it. And just see what happens. (I'm not suggesting you do anything dangerous or reckless though.)

Above all, happy men and women know that happiness begins on the inside and radiates outwards. That's why they attract so much into their lives. Unhappy people believe fervently that happiness is outside, and must be given to them.

For happy people, looking after themselves is a priority. They know that food, exercise and getting enough sleep are critical to their sense of well-being. They make a personal commitment to do what it takes to be physically, mentally and emotionally fit. They schedule quality time to do this each and every week. They always have enough time to do what is important to them.

Genuinely happy people don't overeat and don't indulge excessively in recreational drugs or alcohol. They don't need to. They know that fast food slows them down. So they avoid it. When they are feeling a bit 'down', they also know that the best way of getting themselves out of it is to do something – anything! They don't just sit around the house, moping. They act.

They know how to have real fun and are able to lose themselves in 'play'. It's part of looking after themselves. By ensuring they maintain a healthy work/life balance and manage their energy and stress levels, they don't burn themselves out. They know when to stop. They also know instinctively that being active makes them feel good, whether or not they are aware of the physiology of physical exercise. We feel better after exercise because it releases endorphins into our bloodstreams. These are natural chemicals that serve to make us feel good and positive.

Happy people are action-orientated. They know that even the most outstanding athletes don't win all of the time. By doing more, they inevitably end up getting more and better results. And they are able to set realistic goals and be happy with the results. Not all of these results will be outstanding, but they increase the likelihood that some will be.

Happy people manage to preserve their playfulness, joy and enthusiasm. They don't care if they're not 'good' or accomplished at what they enjoy. They like themselves and feel comfortable with the person they have become over the years.

They are open to the idea of seeing how something works out without requiring a guaranteed outcome from the very beginning. They blame no one and know they can achieve almost anything if they apply themselves to it. Even if they fail, they will have gained something in the attempt. Happy people also laugh a lot. Often at the most ridiculous things. They see the absurdity in everything. And they are not afraid to look or act ridiculous themselves from time to time. They feel good about themselves, they are not too worried about what others think.

They have learned to enjoy the 'now'. Happiness is made up of lots of little moments. They don't expect to feel joy all the time. They go with the flow, accepting reality and life for what it is, not what it could or should be. They don't always need to be right, and willingly accept that they don't have a monopoly on all good ideas. They listen to the opinions and views of others without feeling threatened. They are also open to feedback, which they take without resorting to defensiveness.

They become what they do and what they think about. They have 'good intentions' in everything they do and wish harm on no one.

They always look for, and see, the good in others. Without needing to keep score, favours are given freely with little or no expectation of 'repayment'. Happy people are always happy for other people's success, and are proactive about helping others to feel happy. That in itself makes them happier, too. They always seem to have time for others and actively collect friends and happy memories. They are generally relatively uncomplicated. What you see is what you get. They have no hidden agenda and don't feel the need to impose rules on anyone else. If they have to reprimand someone, they do it respectfully, kindly and in private.

They refuse to beat themselves up emotionally and just concentrate on being and doing the best they can. At the same time, they don't squander their own time with people who consistently drain them. They firmly but politely minimise their interactions with negative people. They have learned to protect themselves against toxic people and poisonous influences.

Generally, they feel good about themselves and who they are, regardless of what shape or size they may be. If that shape or size starts to bother them enough, they accept the responsibility to do something about it.

These are the people who love their jobs and would probably do it for free because they aren't driven by money. Even when they don't love their jobs, they accept their situation and do their best without complaint. Prepared to give more than they gain, they invariably find they receive more than they expect.

And when it comes to love, even though they may have been hurt in the past, they aren't afraid to love unconditionally. The potential gain is worth more to them than the possible pain.

For happy people, life is easier. Less stressful. They accept reality. They see the good in others. They're not overly suspicious, they don't make demands of others, they don't make mountains out of molehills. They don't major in minor things. Little things don't matter. It may have become a cliché, but they really do see the glass half full and not half empty. They don't feel the need to say bad things about anyone.

Every happy person I have ever met likes themselves and they have learned that when they feel good about themselves, just about everything around them takes on a more pleasant appearance.

Everyone can make a decision to be happy right now – in this moment. So focus more on what makes you feel happier.

- Who are the happiest people you know?
- What is it they are happy about? Don't guess. Ask them.

Finish the end of this sentence: *"I am at my happiest when..."*

If it helps, create a fuller list in a journal. In really simple terms, if you want to be happier, do a lot more of what happy people do, a lot less of what unhappy people do! Develop these habits from today.

what you need to know about:

being a kind man

Kindness is SO uncool, especially for a man. Is it possible for a real man to be kind? Or is a kind man, by definition a 'weak' man?

Everyone wants to benefit from the kindness of others, yet being a kind man is instantly seen as a sign of 'weakness'. You simply can't be macho and kind. Or can you? Are kind people weak or strong?

Suppose you are feeling really grumpy. How easy would it be to take out that grumpiness on any innocent bystander? Perhaps someone you claim to care about. By contrast, how strong would someone need to be in order to ensure that they didn't let their grumpiness infect that same innocent bystander? Being grumpy to people who are innocent is simply self-indulgent and disrespectful no matter how you try to justify it.

Practising kindness and compassion is far more difficult, especially if or when you are stressed, tired or irritable. It can require a lot of effort, commitment and self-discipline not to spread how bad you feel to those who don't deserve to suffer. It really is so much easier not to bother. Just bite off the head of anyone who comes within snarling distance of you. How appealing do you think this type of behaviour is? Do it regularly and you will lose friends. It's as simple as that.

Is your bad temper what you really want others to remember about you?

In his book *Why Kindness is Good For You*, author David R Hamilton PhD, cites a study of 10,047 young people aged 20 to 25 from 33 different countries. The research found conclusively that kindness was more attractive than good looks or financial prospects. This applied to men and women. In short, being kind makes you more appealing to others. The personal health and well-being benefits to yourself are also quite compelling, as we will discuss as part of this Emotional Core component.

what is kindness?

The other three pillars of your Emotional Core, self-esteem, attitude and happiness, are mainly about what is inside you. Your attitude will, of course, have an impact on others, and your happiness may be contagious, but these effects are a by-product (albeit an important by-product) of your emotional fitness level. Kindness, on the other hand is outer-directed. It's about others. It's the way you express your emotions to yourself and everyone you know and meet. It is a point of view that effectively says, *"This person exists. They deserve my attention, my respect and even my support."* Whoever they may be.

Who do you know who you would describe as kind? What do they do that makes you think that way about them? I'll bet it involves how they treat everyone they meet, not just those who are 'important'. A true act of kindness so often creates a deep connection with the recipient of that kindness. It means even more to the recipient when the giver has no personal agenda. They are just giving with no desire or expectation of anything in return from that person. Kind people benefit in other ways. So, how kind are you: to yourself and others?

you first

How much do you criticise yourself? How often do you tend to say negative things to yourself that you would never dare say to anyone else? Why do you do this? Putting yourself down is never kind to yourself, even if you've managed to fool yourself into believing it's a way of ensuring others don't think you have an overinflated ego. Attacking ourselves, before we give anybody else the chance to, is a common behaviour amongst people who have yet to learn that being kind to yourself is an essential element of being kind to others. You are not more deserving of criticism than others.

Before you can be kind to others, you must be kind to yourself.

Being kind to yourself is not just about the way you treat yourself emotionally. It is about being kind to yourself physically, as well. If you were a high-performance car, how well would you run on low-quality fuel? Pretty poorly. Stuffing our faces with junk food is not an act of kindness to ourselves. Too many late nights followed by early mornings may be great fun at times, yet an ongoing lack of sleep is not being kind to yourself either.

It's a cliché, but often those who truly value their health are those who have lost it. Looking after your physical body makes sense on a logical level – but why is it that so many of us have been conned into believing that the best way to have fun is to do harm to our bodies?

Millions run their most prized possessions, their bodies, on low-quality, although highly-convenient, rubbish. Fast food makes you slow. Poor quality food really does make you sluggish. What you eat and drink affects your mood and emotional well-being. Eat and drink crap and you'll feel like crap.

How often do you wake up feeling exhausted in the morning? How late do you go to bed? Our bodies require sleep. Living on just a few hours of it is not a sign of strength. Constant tiredness, even among the young, is now extremely common. It affects the speed and clarity of our thinking. And treating your physical body unkindly affects your moods, emotions and general sense of well-being. Everything is linked.

now others

Think about how all of this unkindness you are showing yourself affects you. How likely would it be that someone running their lives in this way would be capable of kindness and be compassionate to others? It's not that likely, is it?

Looking after yourself properly (which isn't the same as being narcissistically self-obsessed) actually increases the likelihood that you'll treat others with more kindness. Think of the people you know who are not kind. They are almost certainly self-obsessed, selfish and inner-directed, sometimes in the extreme, aren't they?

why bother?

Male or female, just about everyone craves intimacy, kindness and being cared for. *"We are actually genetically wired to be kind. This is why it is good for us. And it is also why, when we don't show kindness, or compassion, gratitude or forgiveness, it stresses our nervous systems and is not so good for our health."* writes kindness expert David R. Hamilton PhD.

Being kind to others makes us feel good too. It's a loop. The health benefits include alleviating the symptoms of depression, hurt, stress, anger and anxiety. Doing good, and being good also improve self-esteem. This is another example of how the components of our Emotional Core work together to nourish our overall well-being.

There is a clear link between how happy you are and how kind you behave. Happy people are nice to others, and being nice to others reinforces our happiness. There's that loop again.

A positive, caring attitude has also been found to lead to a longer life. Not only that, kindness is absolutely free. If you're prone to feeling a bit down or depressed occasionally, the most effective way to get you out of it, is to do something kind or helpful for somebody else. Without any expectation of anything in return. Doing so also gives you more energy, which in turn helps you feel more optimistic. Our brain produces the hormones serotonin and dopamine when we are kind. These natural chemicals act on our brains by also improving our optimism. Optimism in turn tends to make us more generous – not necessarily with money, but generous with our time and energy. These are all qualities that make you more appealing to others.

By learning to be kinder and more gentle with yourself, you start to radiate those qualities to those around you. When you understand the bigger picture of kindness, it isn't about you, it's about helping others feel great about themselves. Which doesn't just help them, it lights you up inside, too. People pick this up about you, even if they are not consciously aware of it. The kindness feedback loop is very real and incredibly powerful.

Perhaps it's because random acts of kindness don't tend to make the news, so they stand out in real life. It's a sad reflection of our society's priorities that the more uplifting aspects of human behaviour invariably get pushed into the shadows by the news media, in favour of a constant stream of cruelty, brutality and inhumanity.

how to be kind and compassionate

Think briefly of all the people who have done you wrong, cheated or deceived you. Perhaps you even hate some of them. When you hate somebody else, it only hurts you. Many people find it very difficult to let go; our bruised egos refuse to 'let them get away with it'. So we hold on to those deep, painful emotions. We so often fail to realise that forgiveness is a liberating experience. To forgive someone doesn't mean you have to like them or make friends with them. Forgiveness helps you. It helps you to become less resentful. It clears away dark clouds from the past.

Who could you forgive for whatever they did to you in the past? May be an absent parent? Do it today and notice how a great weight gets lifted from your shoulders. Forgive them whilst expecting nothing in return. They may not understand, they might not even care, but that's OK. You're doing it to be kind to yourself.

Most people are doing the best they can. So learn to be more patient and tolerant. Just because someone may fall short of your standards, it doesn't make them a bad person. Spot people doing good things and let them know you noticed. Help more people in your life to feel special about themselves. Learn how to let out what makes you special so others appreciate you more. The simplest and most effective way to do that is to help others let out their specialness first.

Try developing another new habit of doing at least one kind deed every day without the recipient of your kindness or anybody else knowing. Notice how it makes you feel so much better about yourself. It is the most delicious feeling in the world to know that you've made somebody else's life on that day just a little bit better, without needing to be recognised or thanked for it. In a journal you might like to write down what you did and how these kindnesses made you feel about yourself. Rereading these notes in the future may help you remember what a good person you are.

Make a decision to give at least three genuine and sincere compliments to family, friends, colleagues and even some strangers every day.

Devote yourself to becoming a gold medal Olympic listener. Really listen. If you have to, bite your tongue until the other person finishes. That's not to say that you become everybody's 'audience'. Listening makes people feel special. Give people your undivided attention. Make them realise what they're saying is important to you. Encourage others (especially the quiet types) to open up. Be interested. Look for the good in others and you'll find it in yourself.

Notice the 'invisible' people. I once read an article about a homeless man who talked about the worst aspects of his situation. He didn't want to beg, so he spent hours trying to sell copies of The Big Issue, a newspaper now sold by homeless people all over the world. In the article, the homeless man remarked that over 90% of the people who passed by would look through him as if he wasn't even there. I'm not saying you must always buy a copy, but see the person. Acknowledge the existence of everyone. A smile costs nothing. In Africa, there's a traditional greeting *"I see you."* This means far more than

"Hello." It's about recognising and respecting that person at a much deeper level.

Imagine what it must be like to be the other people in your life. Appreciate the difficulties they experience. Empathise and understand. Always practise good manners. Simply say *"Please"* and *"Thank you"* more often. This is such basic stuff that gets ignored by so many. Yet politeness is free.

penalties and risks of being 'too' kind

Can you be 'too' kind? Yes. Being a 'people pleaser' who is too accommodating and considerate can have a negative longer-term effect. Others may learn to take advantage of such generosity. You may be seen as 'weak' if they think you are prepared to say *"Yes"* to every request. Learn to say *"No"* when it's appropriate. Being kind is not the same as always agreeing to others' wishes.

Recognise and accept that you will be more appealing to some of the wrong people, but also to the right people. So be aware of the risks but don't let it stop you from improving the quality of life for those you know and care about. And listen more to your gut instinct. If you sense that someone is trying to take advantage of you, don't let them.

So, you might be thinking, if this is going to happen, doesn't it make sense to avoid being kind and compassionate in the first place? This way you protect yourself. No. The benefits of being a kind and compassionate person far outweigh any possible disadvantages.

Kind people have become something of a rarity in this dog-eat-dog world. Be that person. But gently insist that any other person in your life needs to be, too.

what I wish I'd known about:

relationships with others

The most significant opportunities in your future life will almost certainly come about as a direct or an indirect result of who you meet and get to know. And (very importantly) who they know.

For others to recommend you, they need to know, like, trust, value and respect you as a man. Why? Because no one these days can afford to put their own reputation on the line by recommending someone who will (or could) let them down.

Therefore, who you get to know in the years to come is incredibly important to you regardless of what you may think at the moment. And starting right now.

However, the biggest problem most people face (and this includes even the most senior, highly experienced men and women) is that nearly everybody feels very uncomfortable about starting conversations with people they don't yet know. And walking into a room of strangers frightens the hell out of a lot of people. In my talks on this subject, I usually joke that it's the fault of our mothers because who hasn't had it drummed into them from an early age *"Don't talk to strangers! It's dangerous!"*

As we all get older, this is something we really need to re-think. We must all learn to talk to more strangers because it's good for business, our careers and our love lives (although clearly, going up to a stranger just for a chat late at night in a dark alley is not usually a good idea!).

We all realise the need to meet new people, but often feel gut-wrenchingly awkward about doing it and will go out of our way to find ways to appear 'too busy' to initiate conversations. We don't know what to say. We worry about what people will think of us. We worry about being rejected, and, of course, there's 'no point' because we can't ever remember anybody's name anyway!

If this describes you – guess what? All of these 'afflictions' are more common than you would imagine. If you are a sufferer – trust me – you are in the majority. Therefore, there is nothing wrong with you.

Get over it. Really. This is so important for your future success. Learn to become more comfortable meeting new people. It is a fundamental life skill that you will benefit from for many decades to come.

The most successful people are almost always the best connected. With excellent connections you will hear about employment opportunities first. You don't get to the top, other people put you there. As your career develops, qualifications and intelligence aren't always enough to reach the top or achieve your career goals. Your ability to relate and connect with others is just as important, if not more so. Every time you meet someone new, your access to potentially valuable new contacts is multiplied by the number of people they know.

Some like to believe that technology can and does replace the need to meet 'real' people. I don't agree. You can never fully replace meeting people face-to-face. Social online media is now so wide-spread, millions interact more with their 'friends' virtually than they do face-to-face. It feels 'safer'. I call it 'arms-length intimacy'. However, technology is a fantastic way to re-connect with people.

Today and tomorrow 'know-who' is and will be more important than 'know-how'.

If you're looking to meet someone for a more personal relationship, it's all about letting a large network know that you're available.

So – from now on, before you go out, or attend your next party, decide not to spend all your time only with the people you know. Promise yourself that you'll start at least one conversation with someone you don't yet know.

A great way to put yourself in the right frame of mind is to think of every stranger you ever meet, from today on, as having the potential to be your next best friend, whether they're male or female. It doesn't matter. So get out more! Just do it.

Here's your first task to improve your confidence. It's fun and you'll learn that it's so easy. Although you might feel a bit self-conscious at first. That will disappear really fast.

When you see someone in the street, in a coffee shop or a bar put a big smile on your face. And just say *"Hello"* in a very warm, friendly and upbeat way as you pass them by. That's all you do. You don't have to stop to have a conversation with them. Just carry on walking. It's really that simple. Give it a go. Do it regularly. Make it part of your daily life. You'll discover that in most cases, they will smile back and say *"Hello"* too. Some won't because they're grumpy gits! It's their problem. Not yours.

Making this part of how you interact with others will help you overcome any shyness or reluctance you might have about meeting new people. Set out to achieve a target to meet, say, three new people per day and increase this number as your confidence and/or expertise grows.

Who knows, you might find yourself saying *"Hello"* to more fantastic looking girls and women. Life can be so tough, can't it?

Walking into a room of strangers can be intimidating to anyone. If you feel particularly uncomfortable about it you're less likely to go out of your way to get into such a position. Avoiding rooms full of strangers may protect you from feeling uncomfortable, but it won't help you meet new people. When you do put yourself through such potential torture, it's very easy to give the situation far more attention and importance than it deserves. But keep in mind that you are not alone: a huge proportion of people feel uncomfortable around strangers. Odds are five out of every six people you see at any party feel equally uncomfortable.

Focus on putting other people at their ease. By choosing to act as a 'host', regardless of whether it's your party or not, you become actively concerned not with your own discomfort, but with ensuring the comfort of others. This helps you forget about your own feelings of discomfort.

Look for people standing on their own and set yourself the task of helping them to feel better about being there.

Here's a tip to overcome extreme shyness: take on the qualities of the people you admire for their confidence and charisma. By 'acting' like them you acquire those positive traits for yourself. It works; give it a go. No one need know that it's an act.

How confident you feel and how confident you look are not the same. Even if you don't feel particularly confident you can appear confident. Learn to stand upright with your feet slightly apart. Don't fold your arms, or cover your mouth with your hand. Make eye contact with those around you and have a smile on your face – this doesn't mean you must grin like a Cheshire cat. Be welcoming, not intimidating. Send out signals that you would welcome a conversation with others. This will increase the likelihood it will happen.

Stand up. Sitting down won't help you meet people.

And finally, learn to enjoy it!

If you'd like to know more about this topic, download my free eBook *Meet Greet and Prosper* which this chapter has been based on. There's a link to it at www.DearSonBook.com/MGP

what I wish I'd known about:

women

"Here's all you need to know about men and women: women are crazy, men are stupid. And the main reason women are crazy is that men are stupid." George Carlin, comedian.

Rule 1. You will NEVER understand women. We are probably not supposed to.

Rule 2. Women always have the final say in an argument with a man.

Rule 3. Anything he says after that is merely the beginning of the next argument!

One chapter in any book could never cover the subject of women in any comprehensive way. Therefore, it would be impossible to do so here. Nor is it remotely possible to accurately describe the sheer variety and complexity of women. This in itself is what makes them so adorable and at the same time so utterly impossible to figure out!

That said, if you want to be able to get on better with women, the next few pages will attempt to explain some of the key differences between how men and women think and behave. If you want to know more on the subject, read any books by Allan and Barbara Pease. Start with *Why Men Don't Listen & Women Can't Read Maps*.

how women talk

There's the story of the young boy who goes to his dad and asks him a question. The dad is preoccupied reading the newspaper. He suggests that the boy go to ask his mother instead. The boy then says in sheer frustration, *"But dad – I don't want to know **that** much."*

Women do tend to talk more than men. Often a lot more. Two guys can go fishing for the day and barely speak to each other but have a brilliant time together. Maybe it's a prehistoric thing. When men went out to hunt, you couldn't chat and stalk at the same time. It would frighten the animals away. Silence was essential. This may also be why men tend to be better than women when it comes to gauging speed, distance, space and trajectories. Now you know why football is such a male dominated team sport. It uses similar hunting skills. Men also tend to have better night vision than women for the same reasons. (That said, any particular woman may be a great runner, hunter or football player: don't insult her by assuming you'll always be better. She has ways of making you pay!)

Men 'report talk' while women 'rapport talk', according to Deborah Tannen, author of *You Just Don't Understand*. Report talking is about saying as much as possible with the least number of words. Using the correct word is important to men. It demonstrates clarity of meaning and focus. Short sentences are manly. Like this one.

For a man, the telephone is a tool to exchange facts. It is not for gossiping for hours on end about (seemingly) nothing. Women see such conversations as strengthening the connections in the relationship.

It's rapport talk. Historically, while men were away hunting, the women would look after children and each other. Building rapport, trust and closeness with people was therefore an essential part of her history, too. Women have no difficulty doing lots of things at the same time. That includes conversation topics.

Women are so good at conversation that they can even run separate ones simultaneously. Women know this. Men get totally confused. It's very common for a man to think, *"What is she talking about now? I'm completely lost."* We can't keep up.

How often have you been listening to a woman and find yourself asking yourself, *"How long is it going to take her to get to the point?"* We really don't want that amount of detail, or all those diversions. And of course there are all those people you don't know that she insists on telling you all about. The point is – she might not have a point. If she likes you, she just wants to keep talking to you. If she's hot, this is a very good sign!

Men tend to function best when we do one thing at a time. And that includes sticking to one point when we're talking. Because men know this, men tend not to interrupt other men. But women can't contain themselves. They will interrupt all the time – but they don't see it as interrupting. To a woman it's proof she's engaged, and wants to be a part of the conversation. But if you ever do the same to a woman – she'll see it as interrupting her! This should give you some idea of how complicated women can be!

When men are interrupted, we just forget what we're trying to say!

I have a friend with five sisters. It's no surprise he became a professional speaker. He has found the perfect job. He can talk uninterrupted for an entire hour. And get paid for what he thinks.

Men do talk a lot of course – but most of it is to ourselves internally. We are constantly thinking about solutions to problems, personal or work-related ones. Women see men being quiet and assume they are unhappy. That's because when a woman goes quiet she is unhappy. A man can be very happy quietly thinking about his stuff. The blank 'gazing in the fire' type of expression on his face doesn't mean he's upset.

Here lies another problem. She assumes he's 'doing nothing'. So she tries to talk to him! It's an interruption. To compound things she also gives him things to do – because she believes he's not doing anything!

That's how women get it wrong with men. Here's how we make a monumental mistake with women, as described by John Gray in his book *Men are From Mars Women are From Venus*. Men have the capacity to put their problems on hold. Women don't. She talks about them. When a woman wants to talk about her problems, she just wants to be heard. She does not want those problems to be solved by you. You absolutely must keep your mouth shut. Say nothing but be seen to listen. To demonstrate this, stop whatever you are doing. Women know that men can't multitask. Therefore, if you're doing something else you are proving that you're not listening to her. So give her your undivided attention. Look at her. Be seen to listen. Develop listening skills – especially with women.

Women often accuse men of not listening. It's not true of course. However, the real problem for men is that there is often too much to listen to!

Let her finish (however long it takes – it could be a while) then do not offer a solution unless she specifically requests one. Keep quiet, especially at times when it's obvious to you what she needs to do.

Finding solutions to problems is what men do well – but don't do this with a woman. She won't appreciate it. In fact, she may even resent you for it. If you were to offer a perfect solution to her – she is likely to feel worse about herself for not thinking of it herself. Even though you've helped her, you've managed to make her feel stupid!

You've been seen to listen. That will make her feel better. You could ask her what she has decided to do about it. Again don't offer any alternative solutions unless she asks for them.

Let's assume you've managed to keep quiet and you didn't force a solution on her. Well done. It's difficult sometimes. The second massive mistake you could make would be to say the following:

"It's not really that important, I don't know why you're letting yourself get so worked up about it." She will hate you for saying that. Never invalidate or belittle her feelings. Her feelings are at the core of who she is. She is upset. To tell her that her feelings don't matter is an insult to her. She will not see it as being helpful, even if you think you're being supportive. (Think about how you would feel if the roles were reversed: you go to the trouble to talk to her about something major, and her response is that it isn't important so don't worry about it. You wouldn't like that, either.)

These differences in conversation styles often cause huge problems between men and women. By understanding these differences, you will be at a real advantage in your dealings with women.

On the plus side, if a woman wants to talk to you it is a clear sign that she likes you. In some ways it doesn't matter what she says, if she's happy with you, she just wants to talk. Many women think out loud. Men tend to do this less than women. With a lot of women there are no filters. No editing. You need to cut through everything to hear what she's saying. Even then most guys get it totally wrong. What a woman says and what she means can be incredibly different. For example, you're walking along the street with a woman. She asks, *"Would you like a coffee?"* You've just had one, so you say *"No."* She gets upset. Why? Because when she asked if you wanted a coffee, what she was actually trying to tell you was that **she** wanted a coffee! It's highly possible that she doesn't want a coffee either, but just wants to sit down with you to talk! Women can be infuriatingly subtle for a man. But she actually expects you to understand the meaning behind what she says - not the actual words.

A woman may say *"could you"*, *"would you"*, *"would you like to"*. To a man, that sounds as though you're being given a choice. They are not choices, they're requests. But a man will say *"yes"* because, he's literal. Yes, he 'could' do it. He hasn't said he will. However, the woman perceives his *"yes"* as a commitment to him doing it. If he then doesn't do what she believes he promised to do, he's then labelled unreliable or lazy. He becomes frustrated and irritated by her wrong interpretation of what she understood.

Before you decide that women are wrong to take this approach, consider this: women who run businesses are statistically far more successful than men because they build such a fantastic rapport amongst their teams. A lot of old-fashioned men think that women just aren't strong enough because they're not telling people what to do. In reality, women are far more effective in getting things done by using cooperation.

Here are a few common words you will hear a woman say – and what they really mean. Do not take these words at face value.

Fine. If a woman says things are 'fine', things are very definitely not fine. She disagrees with you. And is ending the conversation. You will pay later.

Nothing. As in *"nothing's the matter"*. There is something the matter.

Go ahead. This is not permission. She's daring you. Don't go there. You will also pay later.

Whatever. You are history if she says this regularly. You just don't know it yet.

what women like to hear

Make a mistake. Say *"Sorry"*. Mean it.

Ask her lots of open questions. Show genuine interest in what she tells you. These words are always good *"Please tell me – what do you think?"* Ask her *"How much do you enjoy being a woman?"* *"What do you like so much about it?"*

If you are giving her a compliment, be specific. Tell her precisely why she deserves the compliment. *"You look nice."* won't mean a thing to her. But if you said, *"Those ear rings work perfectly with your eyes/your outfit. Where did you get them?"* she will appreciate you noticing the effort she has made. Therefore, pay more attention to her.

banter

Some women like men to think that they can be one of 'the lads' and will often take part in male banter. They want to be liked, to build rapport. But be careful. Good banter among men invariably escalates. It quickly becomes extremely crass and cruel. Cruel words, even when they're harmless fun to a guy, can be deeply upsetting to a woman. Learn when to draw the line with a woman, and draw it sooner than you would with a mate. Many men have been totally confused when one minute you're having great banter, and then out of the blue she bursts into tears 'for no reason'. Now you know the reason. Don't escalate banter with a woman. You may win the banter, but you will lose in other ways.

> "Men socialise by insulting each other, but they don't really mean it.
> Women socialise by complimenting each other, but they don't really mean it either!"
> Anonymous

mocking women

Don't make jokes at the expense of a woman. Definitely not the one you are with. Nor about other women. She will define you as a cruel man. What you also need to understand is that she's not cruel if she says anything unkind about any other woman. She will describe that merely as 'being a woman'.

shopping with a woman

If you ever find yourself cornered into having to go shopping with her (it will happen one day!), as a guy, I advise you to politely decline the offer. But sometimes you sort-of have to go. It's the price you pay for female company. However, it is OK for you to say that you'll go and then set a time limit of, say, two hours maximum.

If you do decide to go, you have a choice: you can tag along, feeling and looking bored listening to your music player (which is unlikely to impress her), or you can use it as an opportunity to learn something useful.

In particular, pay close attention to why she puts clothes back on the rack. Ask her in a friendly way why she decided not to buy something. You will start to understand the complexity of how women think. Trying to understand, she'll feel you care.

when she does finally ask for your advice

Every man has, at some point been asked this question, *"Does my bum look big in this?"* You must learn how to handle this question. A straight *"yes"* is never a good idea. She probably won't accept a straight *"no"* either. You could say, *"I always enjoy looking at your bum. Thank you for giving me the opportunity to study it more closely. Would you mind if I take my time?"* Pause then say, *"It looks great/fantastic/gorgeous!"* And yes, there are times when telling white lies is the best option!

During my conference talks I have often asked if there are any young guys present who have recently been married. If there are, I go on to ask how they would handle the following situation:

You are about to go out together and she asks you, *"Which dress should I wear – the blue one or the red one?"*

Invariably most young guys fall into the trap she's set by giving her his opinion. That was a mistake, to be expected from an inexperienced man. I then open it up to the rest of the audience and invite older, wiser men (who wear the emotional scars of having learned this lesson the hard way) to share how they would answer her trick question. Here are some of the correct answers:

> *"Which dress makes you feel most comfortable?"*
> *"Have you chosen your shoes yet?"*
> *"Why have you chosen them?"*
> *"Which dress goes best with them?"*
> *"Wow, what a great choice."*

She wants to be reassured that she'll look fabulous. Help her to feel good.

This leads to the single most valuable advice you can apply to every woman you ever meet for the rest of your life.

how to really impress a woman

Dear Son
Don't ever try to get a woman to think more of you. You will impress her far more by focusing your energy into sincerely helping her feel better about herself.

Make her feel good about herself. Women don't like men who talk about themselves all the time. They find it arrogant. Men often resort to doing this when they can't think of anything to say. Because we know a lot about the topic, we can speak confidently on the subject for hours on end! Resist the temptation. No woman wants to be part of your audience.

buying gifts for women

Generally speaking, the more practical the gift, the less it will be appreciated. There are exceptions. A female friend of mine was once given a wheelbarrow and she loved it. This is rare. If your gift is for the kitchen, you may end up being forced to wear it. If she describes your gift as *"nice"* she actually hates it.

buying clothes for a woman

Don't. Buying her lingerie is a double don't! Her boobs are smaller than you remember. And her bum is bigger. Therefore neither will fit. You lose points for making her feel bad on each count. She'll not appreciate being reminded about the size of her boobs or her bum. And if you choose bright red, it is highly likely you'll also succeed at making her feel 'cheap'. Therefore, she will hate you too!

If you choose to ignore the advice about not buying her clothing, the secret is to pay attention. When she says how much she likes something, make a mental note of it for later use.

The single most important thing about giving a woman a gift is the thought you put into choosing it. A genuine woman isn't too worried about how much it cost. Flowers from the local service station won't impress her, though.

The next most important aspect of giving a gift to a woman is how much care and attention you put into wrapping it. Really. I learned this lesson when a woman I knew had a 'big' birthday. I bought her a present and wrapped it nicely. When she received it, she burst into tears. I didn't know what to do. I thought, "*OMG, I must have made a huge mistake (somehow),*" so I apologised. She wiped away the tears and said, "*You don't understand. I love it. Thank you so much.*" I asked why it had made her cry. She said, "*Yours was the only present I have received that had been wrapped. All the others were given in carrier bags!*"

Women really appreciate the thought you put into making a gift special.

That's enough about the differences between men and women. More than anything in the world, women, like men, want to be noticed and appreciated sincerely. Learn to appreciate her differences. Notice more. This will help you become more alert to those times when she is playing games with you. It's part of the fun when you're with a genuine woman. However, sometimes women are not genuine. In fact some can be quite dangerous. You must know how to spot them early. Unwary guys first discover their tactics after it's too late. That is the subject of the next chapter.

what I wish I'd known about:

dangerous women

Mothers are usually brilliant at spotting potentially dangerous girlfriends. Unfortunately, as many of them discover, saying anything to their son is a waste of time because he won't listen. Asking a dad what he thinks is pointless too. If she's hot, he'll probably just imagine what she's like in bed, and ask himself why it was that girls never looked that good when he was young.

I have two friends who are both single mums with young sons. One of those sons had a girlfriend who her female instinct told her was bad news for him. She didn't realise just how bad she was until it was too late. The girlfriend had manipulated and cheated the son into taking out loans in his name for her. He went into debt for about £25,000 ($40,000). Then she dumped him and left him with that debt! He was only twenty and faced the prospect of having to declare himself bankrupt.

My other friend's son was also in a relationship with a girl who abused him. He just took it because he 'loved her'. The mother tried to talk to him, but he wouldn't listen. Then she decided to leave on the coffee table, a copy of one of my previous books, *That Bitch*, which is about how to spot dangerous women. It sat there for a couple of weeks. Then one day, it disappeared. He'd taken the bait!

About a week later, he walked into the kitchen and said, *"You know that book of yours by your friend? I borrowed it. I have finished with her. I'll never make the same mistake again. Thanks mum."*

This chapter includes extracts from that book which I co-wrote with Mary T Cleary, who set up a charity in Ireland called Amen.ie for male victims of domestic abuse by women.

Some women don't want a boyfriend or husband – they want a pet! Someone they can control and train to do whatever they want. If she's particularly 'hot' she knows she can find someone who is prepared to be at her beck and call. One of the problems with a lot of men is that we can't help feeling great having an attractive woman on our arm. It tells the world: *"Look at me, aren't I clever/cool to be able to attract a woman as good-looking as this."* In reality, it's possible that she's identified you as a chump.

Unscrupulous 'takers' are fantastic at making you feel sorry for them (often when they absolutely don't deserve it). And they'll milk someone's generosity for as long as they can get away with it. Once found out, they simply move on to their next un-suspecting victim. They also rely on the 'giver's' high degree of trust to give them the benefit of any doubts. Indeed it's common for particularly kind people to feel guilty for even entertaining ideas that they are even being taken for a ride! Because a kind person thinks the best of others, he or she is unlikely to suspect they are being 'played'. Here's how to be more alert, without having to lose the kindness that is so important to your Emotional Core.

women to recognise and avoid

The following character types are inspired by an amusing article by Matthew Fitzgerald:

1. **Miss Anne Thrope.** She is angry at everything and everyone. She will turn against you sooner or later. Get out before she does.

2. **Miss Anne Drist.** She hates men, in the way misogynists hate women. Avoid her. Her hatred may be directed at all men, probably following a bad experience with just one man, possibly when she was a child. Sad or even tragic as that may have been, avoid her. She has the capacity to make your life hell.

3. **Miss Take.** Her middle name is 'Gold-digger'. She expects you to pay for everything. What she wants she gets. If she doesn't get it from you, she'll push and push you into submission. If that fails, she'll move on to another willing man. That is, until he figures out what she's up to and stops lavishing money on her. Miss Take has possibly sold a number of engagement rings for 'sentimental reasons'!

4. **Miss Mimi.** Everything is about her. The Mae West quote comes to mind: "*Enough about me. What do you think of me?*"

5. **Miss Mirage.** She appears to be perfect, everything a man could possibly want in a woman. It's a mirage, a carefully constructed ideal of what she thinks he wants. She keeps up the act until she has trapped him.

6. **Princess Lay'er.** Sex is her lure. She uses either the promise of sex or the continuation of sex to get what she wants. Withdrawing sexual favours is a powerful means of controlling a man. If a woman ever uses sex as a weapon, don't marry her. She

may appear to be sexually captivated by you until it no longer serves her purposes. Or she may have insatiable sexual appetites and make constant demands on you, or multiple partners, and any failure to perform could be greeted with humiliation and ridicule.

An attractive woman with a voracious sexual appetite may be something men dream of. But be careful what you ask for. A woman who wants a lot of sex certainly appeals to a man's ego. "*Hey, she wants me,*" he tells himself. But she might not. Some offer themselves in order to be liked, while others just want to control a man. And she may have a desperate need to feel desired. If she has a voracious appetite for sex, it could be an addiction, so she isn't necessarily into you.

Princess Lay'er leads us to the subject of infidelity. The idea may be difficult for a younger guy to accept but a woman with a high libido is more likely to increase her need for sex as she gets older and into her forties. For a man, the opposite is sometimes true. This is not always the case, but you need to be aware that in later life when your energy levels are not what they were, and your job becomes more time-consuming and demanding as you work hard to support a growing family, you may not be as interested in sex as you are today. But if her interest remains strong, there is an increased possibility that she will seek a younger man, or men, to satisfy her sexually. A leading UK divorce lawyer says that at least 60% of the women who see her to explore divorce options admit they are having at least one extra-marital affair, possibly more.

You need to be aware of why you could be the sort of person who is likely to attract women who will try to use you. Particularly nice, gentle, caring guys are their targets. These sorts of men don't like confrontation; they can be too accommodating, too trusting, a bit naïve sometimes and have a tendency to give others the benefit of any doubt. Most importantly, they ignore their instinct, especially if the girl is stunning to look at or is particularly accommodating sexually. If this describes you – you need to be careful. You have been warned.

A 72 year old man shared this advice he had received from his own father 55 years ago: *"Full testicles. Empty brain."* Some things just don't change!

The women we're describing here aren't always consciously aware of what they are doing, while some know exactly what they are up to.

What you will find is that a lot of ice-cold women have perfected the illusion of appearing hot. But how do you tell the difference? Most men can't. The following could help you. Do you know a woman who exhibits the following personality traits?

- She has an extreme and grandiose sense of her own importance.
- She has an assumption of very high levels of her own talent, success, good looks, power and beauty, even when these qualities are absent or would not be recognised by people she knows.
- Does she insist on excessive and constant admiration?
- Does she have a belief that she has a high degree of 'entitlement'? Because she

believes she is special, she demands special treatment

- Does she have extremely selfish, self-serving and arrogant tendencies?
- Does she have a readiness to take advantage of others in any ways she sees fit?
- Does she have an inability to feel empathy for others? Does she find it difficult to love others because a deep love for herself always comes first?
- Is she convinced that others are incredibly jealous of her?
- And would she be described as very 'high maintenance'?

Everyone exhibits a few of these symptoms on occasion. However, if she has most or all of them, she very well may have narcissistic personality disorder (NPD). This is someone you want to avoid caring for, because she almost certainly won't care about you, no matter what she says.

There are other behaviours that can tip you off that a woman may not be all she seems, and that her apparent lovingness is merely a front. How many of the following behaviours apply to a woman you know?

Over time it has become obvious that at the beginning of the relationship she was on her best behaviour. She seemed to be your perfect partner, but have you found that the more she has relaxed into the relationship with you, especially if you married her, the more of the real woman has been revealed? In the safe environment of the marital home, is she now letting out years, or even decades, of anger that she has had to suppress until now?

Does she have intense, even violent, rages that seem to leap out of nowhere? And do these alternate with periods when she acts perfectly normally and is very loving towards you? Do these make it difficult to know where you stand with her? Do you feel she is Dr. Jekyll and Ms. Hyde? Is she a loving, caring woman one moment, and someone so vicious that you barely recognise her the next? Do you wonder which one is real? Do you hope it's a phase that one day will go away but shows no signs of doing so?

Are you walking on eggshells most of the time, knowing that, no matter what you say or do, it will get twisted and used against you?

Are you blamed or criticised for just about everything that's wrong in the relationship, even when the criticism doesn't make much sense to you? And does that make you question whether you are being the unreasonable one – as she constantly tells you?

Do you feel you are on an emotional roller coaster with high highs when things are incredible and fantastic and very low lows, consisting of feelings of despair, depression and grief for the relationship you thought you had?

Do you find yourself concealing what you really think or feel because you're afraid of her possible reaction, and it just doesn't seem worth the confrontation, a horrible fight or hurt feelings that will inevitably follow? Has this become so automatic that you have a hard time even understanding what you think or feel any more?

Are you afraid to ask for things in the relationship because you will be told you're too demanding or there is something wrong with you? Are you repeatedly told your needs are wrong or unimportant?

Do you feel nothing you do is ever right, or when you do manage to do what she wants she suddenly presents new expectations? The rules keep changing and, no matter what you do, you can't win. Do you feel helpless and trapped every time this happens?

Are you constantly accused of doing things you didn't do and saying things you didn't say? Do you feel misunderstood a great deal of the time, and when you try to explain, she doesn't believe you or want to listen?

Are you constantly put-down, yet when you try to leave the relationship she tries to prevent you in a variety of ways? She tries declarations of love, or she promises to change, or she makes implicit or explicit threats such as *"Nobody but me will ever want or love you."*

Do you have evidence of being lied to? Does she violently deny lying and deflect any conversation away from the topic when you raise it, or does she seem to manufacture accusations to 'prove' you are the liar? Do you feel you're being manipulated or controlled?

Do you regularly wonder whether you're losing your grip on reality because she is always putting you down, or denying your right to a point of view? Does she tend to act normally in front of others, so that nobody would believe it if you revealed what was going on between you?

Does she insist that you not have contact with your family or friends?

If she drinks or takes mood-altering drugs, does her behaviour become more erratic and obnoxious?

Is it next to impossible to plan anything, such as a social engagement, because of her moodiness, impulsiveness or unpredictability? Do you find yourself having to make excuses for her?

How often have you tried to convince yourself that this is normal behaviour?

Perhaps you're now thinking, *"Wow, I had no idea that other people go through exactly the same thing as me."* If you are, you might like to know she probably has borderline personality disorder (BPD). Some BPD sufferers also have a history of eating disorders such as anorexia and bulimia. Threats to commit suicide are sometimes carried out. Their extreme fears of abandonment may stem from childhood trauma, yet their irrational, intense behaviour often encourages the very rejection they fear the most. These personality disorders can be devastating for the sufferers. Being in a relationship with one can be worse.

trapped into an early marriage

In this segment we're going to look at some of the ways dangerous women are prepared to trick a man into marrying her.

Women who are serious or desperate to find a husband invariably learn about a book that boasts sales of more than a million copies. It's called *The Rules*. If your girlfriend is in possession of this book, get out. Fast. You are possibly what the authors describe as *'live prey'!*

In fact the authors suggest quite strongly that this is a book that should be kept out of sight. This is why: the book is all about trapping a man to marry him.

To further this aim, she may adopt some of the following tactics:

She will never say or show that getting married is on her mind, even when it is.

She rarely, if ever, calls you or even returns your calls. She wants you to do all the running to make it look as if she doesn't need you or even want you. She wants you to think of her as a challenge. Then further down the line when you've put so much effort into winning her, you will be less likely to dump her.

She's taught to make sure that whenever you are on the phone together she will be the person who always ends the conversation. She always wants to leave you hungry for more.

She makes a point of not answering her phone when you call. This is to create the impression that she's too busy or is in such demand from other men. This might not be at all true but she wants you to think other men want her. The authors of *The Rules* seem to believe that most men will fight harder to win a girl if they think they have competition! She may be deliberately appearing to be emotionally cool towards you to give you that impression.

She is encouraged not to show she is jealous or insecure. She is told to never appear needy, even though she might be an extremely needy individual.

She is advised to never ask you where you've been or who you've been seeing. This helps her perpetuate the appearance of not being too bothered.

She always acts as if everything is great, even if it isn't. In fact, she's told to always look and sound happy and upbeat, even if it's an act.

She will act as if she is independent so that you don't feel she is expecting you to take care of her, even though that is in fact her objective.

She won't agree to see you more than twice a week. She may claim that she's not available even though she is.

She's told that she mustn't ever accept an invitation for a weekend date if you ask after Wednesday of that week. She doesn't want you to think that she can be called last minute.

She learns to gently insist you have to rearrange your schedule around her.

A girl who's read this book is also told to never have sex with a guy until at least three dates.

She's told to dump any guy who doesn't give her expensive romantic presents for her birthday.

She is also advised to not live with you or even leave her things at your place. She wants to condition you to feel that if you want to see her seven days a week, you have to marry her.

If you're in a long-term relationship with a girl who wants to get married, she may claim that she's pregnant. This is sometimes just to see how the guy responds. Genuine accidents do happen, of course. Calmly ask her how she feels about it. When (not if) she asks you how it makes you feel, tell her that you want children only when they are planned. If she pushes you into telling her what she should do about it if she was pregnant, don't be drawn. If she's manipulating you, that is the trap. Politely and considerately say you are prepared to sit down with her to discuss it properly if or when a pregnancy test proves positive.

During the research for this book, I spoke to

a lot of teenagers and young men. In every case, I would hear a story of how one of their school friends was going to have a baby. Accidents do happen. But not all are accidents.

Particularly unscrupulous and dangerous women will deliberately get themselves pregnant if they suspect their boyfriend will do the 'honourable' thing and then ask her to marry him.

Do not marry a woman out of duty or honour if she is (or claims to be) pregnant. If she is pregnant, you must also receive medical proof that the child is yours. DNA testing is essential. If the child is yours you definitely have an obligation towards it. But you don't have the same obligation towards the mother. Perhaps she is the right woman for you, but having a baby is not proof of that.

If any girl exhibits a combination of several of the above behaviours – she's almost certainly working on you. So be really careful.

The book I've been talking about has been described as an approach to manipulate an unsuspecting man into committing himself to a marriage that he thinks was all his own idea. The authors claim that if a girl follows their 'rules' she can rest assured that her husband will treat her like a queen – even when he's angry with her. Because he invested so much time and effort trying to get her in the first place.

The authors claim that when women have followed their recommendations, their approach has led to countless happy marriages. What they don't share is how many marriages they have helped to start that have resulted in misery for everyone, including any children who are produced by this deceitful scheming. Nor do they say whether such an outcome would be in the best interests of any man who is duped by a woman so desperate to get married that she would resort to this type of behaviour.

The book says, *"If you're a genuinely nice person, you will probably feel cruel when you do The Rules. You may think you are making men suffer, but in reality you are actually doing them a favour."* Apparently, playing deceitful games is not bad.

What seems to say it all to me is how they beseech their readers not to tell their therapist about the book. Because the therapist may just believe that such an approach is a manipulative and dishonest way to trap a man into marriage. Surely not!

We've all heard the phrase *"Hell hath no fury, like a woman scorned."* Many of the women we are talking about here just feel scorned. And they are hell bent on taking it out on anyone – male or female. Innocent or guilty. Because they can't quite figure out who has scorned them, 'anybody' will have to do!

Don't let yourself be one of them.

what I wish I'd known about:

marriage & divorce

Dear Son
Please don't get married too young.

Decisions can be difficult at the best of times. Choosing the right woman to marry is one of the most important decisions you will ever make. The last chapters should have made that clear.

Full disclosure: I have made the wrong decision twice. So you might be forgiven for thinking that I'm anti-marriage. Not at all. I'm anti-**bad** marriages! If this chapter stops just one bad marriage from happening, it has to be worth it. Not just for the man but also for the woman as well as any children. In the interest of simplicity, I'll use the term 'marriage' throughout this chapter, but please recognise that what I am saying applies to other types of relationships, too.

Living together without getting married has become the preferred option for many couples. In Scandinavia, for example, it is widely recognised that the institution of marriage is dying. The link between marriage and parenthood has also been broken. A growing number of children are born out of wedlock without social stigma. However, living together still entails the same type of psychological and emotional commitment, and compromise, as a marriage. So even if you don't plan to marry, this chapter still includes important information for you.

The same holds true for same-sex marriages or partnerships: you are committing to another person, and that involves compromise. In most (but not all) cases, same-sex marriages don't include children, but other legal responsibilities associated with straight marriages also apply.

Marry the right woman and both of your lives will be enriched beyond your wildest dreams. Marry the wrong woman and you face the distinct possibility that you will endure a living nightmare. Ask any man who has been divorced to tell you what it was like! Even the best divorces are emotionally draining. You don't want to know about the worst!

If you have been caught up in a divorce as a child, you will know at first hand how difficult life can get. The confusion you felt. Did you convince yourself that it was somehow your 'fault'? Where did your loyalties lie? Did you take sides . . . and with hindsight was that a good idea? Divorce rips lives apart. You need to do everything you can to never get divorced. Of course, one way of avoiding this possibility is to not get married in the first place! But for most people this is not a sensible option.

So what can be done, if anything, to choose your future wife wisely? You might find it helpful to understand the different reasons men and women get married.

why some men marry

Generalisations are never accurate. Even so, here are a few reasons men have given for deciding to get married:

Firstly, there's love. Both are so deeply in love. They were made for each other, true soul mates and best friends. They know each other incredibly well, they have mutual respect for each other and genuinely want the same from life. They have found lasting happiness and will remain together for the rest of their long lives. That's the plan, at least. And many times it works. But not always.

He loves his girlfriend. As she is so keen to get married, many men become GAGs – Go Along Guys. A man like this will propose to show how committed he is to the relationship. This is not a good enough reason to marry.

As discussed earlier, she discovers she's pregnant, so he proposes in a gesture to make an 'honest woman' of her.

He may think that he's starting to feel a little too old for the singles bars he has frequented for a number of years – another sign that it is time for that next phase of life.

If his male friends are starting to get married, he may think he had better do it, too. If not, he could be left on his own.

When a man starts to lose his hair, he often sees it as the first sign that he'd better think about settling down before he becomes too unappealing to women. If the hair loss coincides with packing on a bit of weight, his fear of being left on his own sharpens his mind further.

How old he feels and how old others make him feel will also have an impact on his openness to the idea of marriage.

Perhaps she wants to marry him, so she proposes. He is grateful or flattered that someone wants him.

Or he is incredibly needy, neurotic and desperate for a wife. His emotional core is weak. He believes he can't function without her – so she's the one who has to be convinced.

Most graduates leave university or college with large debts, which take time to pay off. It is not well viewed for a man to marry while in debt. However, society takes a far kinder view of a woman who marries before paying off college debts.

why some women marry

Millions of kind, loving and well-meaning parents tuck their little girls up in bed at night and feed them a daily diet of fairy stories featuring beautiful young girls who meet handsome princes, fall in love, marry and live happily ever after.

Some of these parents even put stickers on their car bumpers or inside their vehicles proclaiming to the world: 'Little Princess On Board'. How many of these same parents are unwittingly creating unrealistic expectations for their daughters in years to come? How many of these innocent little girls start to believe they are princesses? And how many learn, subconsciously perhaps, to expect to be treated like royalty by everyone, especially men – because that's what daddy did?

Marriage is therefore an aspiration for many women from a young age. They are in love with the ideal of what marriage should be, and the notion of having a party in their honour on a day when they will look as beautiful as they're ever going to.

Many women want the status of being a 'wife'. In her mind, it validates her as a woman.

Most people are genetically programmed to want

children, but the tendency seems to be stronger at an earlier age in women than in men. Some women are more determined than others, especially if they reach an age when their girlfriends are marrying in droves. A woman may start to feel that if she doesn't find a man soon, it might be too late to have children. Women from their late twenties and into their mid-thirties become increasingly aware of how loud their biological baby clock is ticking.

And there are 'hitchhiker wives'. These women look for wealthy men, or men they believe have the potential to become wealthy. These men are chosen for their ability to provide a woman with a lifestyle of leisure. She can stop working, have children and spend her life 'doing lunch', going to the gym and shopping with her other hitchhiker girlfriends. All the while, the man is working hard to pay for it all. Should his career suffer, she may get out while she can by filing for divorce. Even though she may have not contributed much to the marriage, she goes to court to take as much out of the marriage 'pot' as possible. This is the equivalent of convincing a judge that even though she was a hitchhiker, she now wants the car she was driven around in because she believes it is now hers! In many cases, a judge will agree! This example might sound absurd, but divorce law often is, when seen from the man's perspective.

Don't ever pick up these types of hitchhiker!

If your girlfriend has made it clear to you that she would like to be married, you must find out why it's so important to her. And what she sees as your role as her future husband.

before you propose

Marriage is mostly about the friendship, love and commitment between two people sharing the good and bad aspects of day-to-day living: cooking, cleaning, ironing, and all the other aspects of running a household. Making joint decisions about where to live, what job to take (and what to do if you lose yours, or she loses hers), what your priorities are and how to pay for them. Deciding on how large, or small, a family you want, when you want to start it, and how you wish to raise your children. And all of these decisions involve another person whose points of view will not always match yours.

For some men or women, early in a relationship, it can appear quite appealing that their partner tends to make most of the decisions. So long as both parties are happy with this it can work well for a long time. However, a relationship can collapse quite quickly if either party starts to resent the other person for doing what they've always done!

Just suppose, your girlfriend sees you as a strong decisive type and is happy for you to make a lot of the decisions. She sees it as a sign that you care about her. But what if, as she gets older, she grows in confidence and starts to resent the fact that you make all the decisions? (It can work exactly the other way around, too.) Her resentment could become a belief that you are being too 'controlling'. This is often cited as a reason why women file for divorce!

I was once told this story: a guy had lunch with an older woman who he knew had divorced her husband for this very reason. She'd told him that he was a 'control freak'. He asked what she'd like to order for lunch. She said, *"You choose for me."* He politely refused, joking that he only did that for four-year-olds. In that moment it became clear (to him at least) that she had almost certainly been responsible for training her husband to make all her decisions. Yet that was one of the main reasons she divorced him!

Conflict and confrontation are natural parts of life. Some people thrive on creating it, while others will agree to almost anything in order to avoid it. Which type are you? Which type is she? If one of you were described as a bit 'bossy,' who might they be talking about?

Some young couples are proud of the fact that they don't argue. This is not necessarily a good sign. It may be because you are 'in synch'. But it may be because one of you chooses not to argue. Swallowing anger or resentment does not make it go away, either on your part or hers. Eventually it comes out.

In addition, you must know how she fights! Is she reasonable, calm, empathetic? How often is she unreasonable? How often does she have tantrums and mood swings? Does she turn on the tears at will? Is she prone to making demands that only take her interests into account? Does she insist on getting her own way? If so, do you give in for an 'easier life'? Or is it the other way around?

Each time anyone avoids confrontation by giving in for an 'easier life', it reinforces the other person's expectation of getting their own way in the future. This is not healthy for any relationship. Give and take is good – but never if it's predominantly one person who does the giving and the other does the taking!

Being married to a woman who has learned to expect to get whatever she wants most, if not all, of the time, could come back to haunt you.

Also consider how she responds when you treat her well. Does she express warm appreciation of such behaviour, or does she just seem to naturally expect it, or does she actually demand it? And how does that make you feel?

What about your attitude towards her? Do you appreciate, expect or demand particular behaviours of her? Have you ever noticed her reaction? Pay attention. Other attitudes you need to pay attention to:

- How self-obsessed is she?
- How does she treat friends?
- Is she kind or cruel to people?
- How does she behave when no one is watching?
- What do your friends really think about her? Ask them seriously. Observe the delay before they say anything. That could tell you a lot.
- Are relatively small things always blown up into full-time dramas by her?
- Does she see conflict as a battle that she must always win? If so, being married to her could get ugly one day.

what is a marriage . . . legally?

Being a loving couple, having children and living happily ever after is the goal of most men and women when they get married. But what is a marriage? It used to be a *"Holy union in the eyes of*

God." That has changed. Your government now runs the marriage 'franchise'. The Church no longer has the same power it used to have.

When you sign a marriage license you accept the terms of your government. It is a legally binding 'business' contract. Most of the contract terms are irrelevant if you stay married. However, if you divorce, how assets are split can have a monumental impact on your finances and your future options. Although the details vary by country, the main clauses are fairly uniform. For example, when you get married all assets are shared equally. A farmer once commented following his marriage, *"I remember walking up the aisle owning a farm, and walking back down the aisle owning half a farm."* Debts, regardless of who incurs them are shared equally. If you marry someone with undisclosed debts, you are still liable for them.

pre-nuptial agreements

If a man dares to suggest to his future wife that they sign a pre-nuptial agreement he risks an accusation of being unromantic and distrustful. But pre-nuptial agreements make enormous sense for anyone (male or female) who own substantially more assets or cash than their partner before marriage. Pre-nups, as they are called, would state that both parties retain full ownership of those assets or cash if the marriage ends in divorce. In other words, no one can take out of the marriage more than they have put in. Pre-nups are not always recognised by the courts, although they are being accepted far more widely than in the past.

Critics of pre-nups claim that they are unfair to

a woman who may be marrying a man with money, because she is prepared to sacrifice her career for the benefit of her husband. However, it is rarely acknowledged by those same critics that the woman already has a pre-nup to protect her own personal interests. It's called a marriage license!

This issue is very controversial. The purpose for including it here is merely to illustrate how seriously you need to consider what you are buying into when you decide to marry.

These are the most sobering facts of all. Just over 50% of all marriages end in divorce. And about 40% of second marriages also fail. 60–70% of all divorces are initiated by the wife. Most of those divorces are announced after months of careful exit planning. In almost all cases, the man gets financially skewered. And if there are children involved, the father may be forced to pay even more, and lose the house he's been paying for so that his ex-wife can live there to bring up the children. Sometimes with a new boyfriend, who may end up having more contact with those children than the biological father, who is often forced to find alternative, lower grade accommodation.

Q. *"How many divorced men does it take to change a light bulb?"*
A. *"No one knows. Men never get to keep the house."*

due diligence

In our book, *That Bitch*, my co-author Mary T Cleary and I created a document called a 'Due Diligence Checklist'. It is equally useful for men and women, and lists many questions to ask each other to uncover any information that either party needs to know before going ahead with a marriage. It deals with attitudes to life, including roles and responsibilities. Numerous married people told us that they wish they'd had those conversations before they got married.

You can download this checklist for free from www.DearSonBook.com/DD. If you know anyone who is planning to get married, feel free to send this link to them.

After reading all this, should you be pessimistic about marriage? Absolutely not. But you should be realistic. Too many people still go into marriage with their eyes closed. They are not aware of what they are getting into. This chapter has been quite 'heavy'. This is not to persuade you to avoid marriage. It's a sincere attempt to minimise the number of bad marriages.

Becoming a couple, whether married or not, is a 24-hour a day commitment. In fact, it is like a full-time, extra-intense friendship. And remember this: friendship is based on warmth. Not on how 'hot' she is!

So choose your wife well. And don't be in too much of a hurry to do so.

what I wish I'd known about:

sex

For religious or other reasons you may have decided not to engage in sex outside marriage, or to have any form of casual sex. If you are sure you will stick to this view, feel free to skip this section.

For the rest of you, this chapter covers what is almost always omitted from formal sex education lessons. You're probably already so tired of hearing about the mechanics of sex: the *"what fits where"* stuff and hearing *"always use a condom"*, *"irresponsible sex gives you diseases"* and *"don't get a girl pregnant"*. As well-meaning (and as critically important and true) as that information is, it doesn't help you to know what to do when you finally find yourself with a girl, perhaps for the first time. You're sort of expected to already know what to do. But it's a bit like wanting to be a master painter before you've ever picked up a paintbrush! Or expecting to be an Olympic Gold medallist at sex the first time you ever 'compete'! (Hopefully it won't be in front of a cheering crowd and this is one time when you don't want to be disqualified for going off too soon, or coming first!)

According to research, a substantial proportion of boys and girls all over the world now learn about sex by watching porn on the Internet. If this describes you, please, please erase what you think sex is all about based on what you may have seen. Porn is definitely sexual, but it is absolutely not 'making love'.

Watching a man who's hung like a donkey banging away at a submissive woman who is being paid to look like she's enjoying it, is not what real sex is about. Nor is it helpful to you or any woman you will ever have sex with. Do not confuse porn with sex. Or confuse sex with lovemaking. Loving sex is not about being submissive.

Pornography is a hugely profitable global business. It is only interested in making money. Free porn is offered purely to persuade (mostly) men to pay for it. Porn is not sex education. And that includes a lot of so-called sex education DVDs.

Sadly, a lot of young women see porn too, and are equally confused about what is expected of them.

If you are serious about becoming a 'good' lover one day – don't ever copy what male porn stars do. Please. But, what do you do instead?

Porn only focuses on one aspect of what turns on a guy. It is about self-gratification. It completely ignores the female perspective. The best preparation you can have for real sexual experience is to gain a better understanding of a woman's sexuality.

If you just thought, "*I don't really care about that*", you'll never be a good lover. It's as simple that. To be 'good' at sex absolutely requires you to know how a woman thinks (of course, you'll never know what she thinks!) and what pleases a woman sexually. That includes physical as well as emotional pleasure. And then being motivated to give her that pleasure – on her terms. Guessing doesn't count either. You can't ever learn any of that from watching porn.

Warning: "*No*" means "*NO*" whenever it is spoken. If she says "*no*" she means it. Don't ever risk getting this wrong. Don't take advantage of a woman under the influence of drink/drugs or get so carried away in the moment that you ever ignore her wishes. The legal consequences could wreck your life.

self-love

Before we explore sex with a partner, for most teenage boys, masturbation, or jerking off, tossing off or wanking as it's also known, plays a central role in their lives. As men get older, it still plays a role, but in most cases it's less so. As the joke goes, "*97% of all men masturbate. While the remaining 3% lie about it.*"

Masturbation is perfectly natural and, contrary to the old wives tale, it doesn't make you go blind. There is nothing to be ashamed of, or to feel guilty about. In fact, it can help you relax, can be comforting, helping you to get to sleep and help you let off the 'steam' associated with normal sexual frustration. You can do it solely for your own personal pleasure without taking into consideration the needs or desires of a partner. Premature ejaculation can be a problem for some men. Masturbation is an effective treatment.

Masturbation is also safe because you don't catch STDs from yourself! Discovering how to give yourself sexual pleasure is part of growing up. So don't worry about doing it. But it's best to lock the door first so you aren't disturbed or interrupted.

However, it's worth being aware of the following: If you're single and not in a sexual relationship – no problem. If you're in a relationship, your partner might feel aggrieved that you feel the need or desire to continue. Can you masturbate too much? Yes. If you end up preferring to masturbate than have partner sex, this can create sexual problems for you and a partner. It is also possible to link sexual stimulation with particular types of hard core, violent porn. People addicted to this type of masturbation, sometimes condition themselves to only get turned on in these ways. This can lead to all sorts of psychological problems.

In a healthy, long-term, trusting sexual relationship, it's common for partners to masturbate in front of, or for each other, to help them learn how their partner gives themselves sexual pleasure.

what women want

Female sexuality is far more complex than it is for guys. It's been said that women need reasons to have sex, while men just need a place!

For a lot of girls/young women it is hugely important what other people will think about her if she 'gives out' too easily. Her reputation is important to her. While on the other hand, she's probably just as curious and as keen to 'play' as most guys. It's very common even for a very attractive woman to feel deeply self-conscious, awkward, even embarrassed about her body. The idea of being naked with someone is potentially very stressful for her. What if she isn't any 'good' at sex? How will she react to seeing her first erect penis? What does she do with it? What if she gets it wrong? What if intercourse hurts? What if she doesn't even like it? What will he think of me?

What are your own 'what ifs'? How hard do you

touch her? Where? When do you go 'there'? What if I don't get hard, or stay hard? It's quite normal to feel uncertain in these and many other ways.

It's possible that she's done it before and has more experience than you. She probably won't want to volunteer that information in case you might think badly of her.

Male or female, our first experiences of sex, and sexual intercourse in particular, can have a deep and very long-lasting effect on our approach to future sexual encounters and relationships. You have a responsibility to yourself and to your partner to make your early experiences positive ones.

Unfortunately, a lot of the time it's not a particularly positive experience for the woman – and deeply stressful for the man. This is mainly because so many inexperienced men and women mistakenly try to copy what they think sex should be from what they've seen in porn movies. For the man, he may be so wrapped up in trying to impress with his staying power, energy and even his acrobatic skills, while she lies there thinking that it isn't what she was hoping it would be. They then both realise (quite quickly) that staying power is a skill he has yet to master – and it's all over. He collapses on top of her with a huge grin on his face thinking he's the master of the universe, while she's thinking, *"Hmm, that wasn't so good."* Or *"I wish I hadn't agreed to this. When is he going to get off me?"*

how to be a great lover
A man's sexual gratification generally centres around his genitals. It's understandable therefore, that an inexperienced man wrongly assumes that a woman's

experience is the same. Her sexual pleasure does not centre around her vagina, clitoris and nipples.

A woman's whole body can be her sexual playground and exploring all of it sensuously, can be an amazing experience for her as well as for you.

Women have been blessed with a multitude of erogenous zones, which perhaps seems a bit unfair to us men! But we have them too and it's OK to encourage your partner to find them as well.

Dear Son
Learn to enjoy a woman's enjoyment.

Giving sexual pleasure to a woman is at the core of being a great lover. In an ideal world, when it comes to sex, almost every woman with or without sexual experience would really appreciate any man who knows the following:

She wants to feel good about herself and reassured in a sincere, genuine way. She wants to feel safe. And be safe. She wants to feel that you care about her and how she feels.

She absolutely does not want to feel under any pressure to do what you want her to do, or allow you to do to her. She wants to feel appreciated and respected. She doesn't want it to hurt. She doesn't want to feel used in any way. Or feel 'dirty' for having done something she later regrets. She doesn't want to feel disappointed. Above all, she wants it to be a positive experience.

This is how you make your early experiences more successful and enjoyable for you and for her.

It's better to stay sober! Some booze can relax you but even slightly too much will detract from the experience. S. L. O. W. down. Don't be in a rush to get to the 'main event'. It is very unlikely indeed you will ever meet a woman who doesn't appreciate having her neck, back, hair, shoulders and stomach being stroked and touched in non-sexual ways. This type of touching can be incredibly relaxing for a woman.

If your partner is someone you know well (which is always the preferred option in the early days of sexual activity because you can both learn together) tell her that you don't want to put her under any pressure and then invite her to let you know when she wants you to do more. You can even gently ask her to take your hand and place it where she'd like you to touch when she is ready. This gives her control of the situation.

By focusing your attention on giving sensuous rather than sexual pleasure to your partner you dramatically reduce the potential for embarrassing premature ejaculation (climaxing too soon) which is a common and very real probability for any young man who is sexually inexperienced or overexcited.

Slow and gentle is much better than 'passionate'. If you misjudge 'passion' it can be perceived as aggression. That isn't good. So slow down and give her pleasure.

Do that and you will be a true master of the universe in her eyes. And don't be surprised if she is also keen to practise with you a lot more often!

what I wish I'd known about:

decision-making

Sick and tired of being told what to do by parents and teachers all the time? It can be so frustrating when all your decisions are made for you. In some ways though, it can be much easier than making your own.

Being taught how to make better decisions isn't very common. Usually we're left to figure it out for ourselves and learn from our mistakes. There is a better option. In this section you'll learn a few techniques that will help you make more good decisions and fewer bad ones. Please note: this does not mean you will never make bad decisions! You will. Hopefully none of them will be fatal, have long-term consequences or be financially crippling.

Here's how to practically guarantee making bad decisions:

- Only consider your short-term needs.
- Only consider the needs of others.
- Only consider how you feel about the situation.
- Ignore the facts.
- Confuse facts with your own assumptions and/or the opinions of others.
- Fall for the 'This once-in-a-lifetime offer is only available for a limited time – buy now or miss out.' Don't allow yourself to be pushed into making decisions in this way

- If you need time to think about something, take that time. Realise that if someone is pushing you to make a snap decision, it's usually a sign that they are putting their needs ahead of yours. It's a very well-known ploy, because it works. Don't let it work on you.

Avoid the list above and you'll make more good decisions. In addition to the above, do more of the following:

Decide to decide things. This in itself is a decision and it builds your confidence. Not making a decision can be a bigger mistake than making bad decisions.

Understand how you currently make decisions. For example, what factors would you consider when choosing which college or university to apply for? The reputation of the institution and/or the tutors? How many years the course is? How near or far it is from home? Whether it is in the centre of a large city, or a quieter backwater campus? How vibrant the social, sport or music scene is? Etc. All these factors are important, but the interesting question to ask yourself is: how much importance do you give each of the factors relative to each other? And how likely is it that the way you tend to evaluate situations will lead to a better decision and to a good longer-term outcome? What might the consequences be if you gave certain aspects of your decision too much importance, or not enough?

From now on, after each decision you make, whether it's big or small, evaluate whether it was a good decision or not. This habit will help improve your 'hit rate' of good decisions. If you find that you are making a lot of decisions you later regret, it can be incredibly useful if you can learn how to uncover any recurring reasons. It could be that you tend to make many decisions too quickly, without thinking through possible or likely consequences. Or, on the contrary, maybe you agonise over every possible possibility, getting stuck in analysis paralysis. Then again, perhaps you are too afraid of what other people think, so you dither over all decisions. Learning to understand your decision-making strengths and weaknesses is a key skill.

Going along with decisions made by others can appear the easy option. In many cases, however, you pay a high price later. So, actively make more of your own decisions and accept responsibility for them. Caring parents may offer to bail you out if you make poor decisions. This is very loving of them, but be aware that knowing they are there as a safety net all the time can lead you to making ill-informed decisions because you are not ultimately responsible for the outcome. The sooner you decide to take full responsibility for your decisions, the sooner you'll take your decisions more seriously. Before you make future decisions learn these habits:

Stop. Step back. Look at the bigger picture. Define the situation. How important is this decision in the short and the longer term? If it's not that important, don't waste too much time evaluating all the options. Ask yourself, *"What else is worth considering?"*

If you can, step into the shoes of any other people who may or will be affected by your decision. If appropriate, ask them for their views or what they want. A great question to ask others is, *"If you* were me, what would you do?" Then ask, "Why?" Tell them you'll consider their position but you need to weigh up all the options before you make your decision. Accept now that not all decisions will be received well by everyone else. As you'll find in years to come, the mark of a leader (even if you are only leading your own life) is the ability to make wise decisions that may be particularly unpopular in the short-term. So clarify your purpose. What do you want to achieve? What are the top priorities, what are the factors that are less important? What are the options you haven't yet thought about? Balance your personal well-being and factor in the importance of your decision to others. Don't only do what's right for you every time. Or what's right for others all the time.

Tossing a coin is not the way to run your life, so here is a technique you can use for a wide range of decision-making situations:

pros and cons

Take a sheet of paper, draw a vertical line down the middle. On one side of the page list all the pros (positives). In the other column list all the cons (negatives). Simply doing this exercise might help you see in black and white what the decision needs to be. If you are still unclear, assign a number from 0 to 10 to each item you have written. The higher the number, the more important it is to you. Then count up all the numbers in each column. Before you make your final decision, take a second look at your scores. Have you based them on facts, opinions or preferences? Understanding this can have a significant impact on your final decision.

It's worth giving a special mention to the role your emotions play when making decisions. The better you understand your emotions, the more likely it will be that your decisions will be made from a firm and stable foundation. This is another reason why you need to strengthen your emotional core, as described on pages 38 to 85.

The next chapter focuses on your attitude towards risk. Risk is an integral part of how you make decisions. It is always worth giving some serious thought about the real and imagined risks associated with your decisions. Do you tend to ignore, overestimate, or underestimate risks? To ignore risk is potentially dangerous. What will, or what could, be the consequences to you or others when making risky decisions?

Ultimately, your life story will be the result of all the decisions that you ever make and those you don't. Therefore, it is worth learning from the earliest age how to increase the proportion of good decisions you make, and minimising your bad ones. On a personal note, I really wish I'd known how to do this stuff much earlier in my own life! It would have made so many things so much easier!

what I wish I'd known about:

risk, responsibility and reputation

risk

Joyriders are a great example of young people (usually guys) who wrongly believe that they have the skill and knowledge to drive at high speed in stolen cars. The adrenaline rush from this high-risk behaviour is more important to them than anything else. But this doesn't make them more 'manly'. Only 'pretend' men behave in reckless, irresponsible ways. No real man would ever risk the lives of passengers, innocent pedestrians or other motorists.

How you make decisions, your ability to delay gratification (remember the marshmallow experiment mentioned earlier) and how addicted you are to the rush of adrenaline associated with risky behaviour are all linked. Taking risks can be exciting. The buzz can be quite addictive. It gives you the feeling that you're so alive, living on the edge.

However, each time you take a reckless risk and get away with it you strengthen your belief that the risk was actually low. This can escalate recklessness, until one day your luck runs out. What you came to believe was low risk, wasn't. Most men and women in prison today are there not necessarily because they are bad people (although obviously a lot of them are), they're there because they have a really poor ability to assess risk. They either believed they would never get caught, or they simply didn't worry about it. Many never stop, even for a moment, to think about any possible consequences to their behaviour. That's fine if they are the only people who are affected by their behaviour. They will be the only ones to pay the price. And when it affects innocent bystanders, it can literally wreck their lives.

On the other hand, accept that everything has an element of risk. Be safe, but don't wrap yourself up in so much cotton wool you smother yourself. Accept that bad things happen. It's called life.

Dear Son
Learn to evaluate all risks accurately. Be bold, but not foolish. Ask her out! Apply for that dream job!

responsibility

Why bother being responsible? Why not do whatever you want, whenever you want? Why pay money to learn to drive? Why pay all that money to get insurance? Why not take the risk?

Being responsible is at the centre of being a real man. It starts with taking full responsibility for your own actions. And all the consequences and rewards that go with that. Professionally, your ability to accept responsibility will be a key factor in your career success. If or when you ever have a family, you'll be responsible for the lives and well-being of your children. Therefore, you may as well get as much practice at being responsible from today.

reputation

I was 15. My dad needed to give me another talking to because I'd said something horrible to my mother (sorry mum). As ever, I wasn't particularly interested in what he was telling me. It was a waste of time for both of us. Then he said something which hit me between the eyes. I remember it as if it was yesterday. He told me that it takes years to build a reputation and only moments to lose it all. He said that our personal reputation was the only thing we have. And added an almost throwaway remark, *"I can walk into any room anywhere, confident in the knowledge that I will never meet anyone I have ever cheated or mistreated. That allows me to sleep at night"*.

Will you be able to do that one day?

Suppose you were applying for an amazing job. You really want that job. What would the potential employer see you getting up to if they searched for photos, videos and comments in places like Facebook? Employers and recruiters do that. They want to know what type of person you are in private, too.

A reputation is the complex result of all the decisions you make (and don't make), what others say about you behind your back, what they are prepared to say about you to influential people on your behalf, how much you are trusted, whether others perceive you as someone who is only interested in what's 'in it for you' or whether you are someone who is occasionally or regularly prepared to go out of your way to help others.

A good reputation will open more doors of opportunity for you. And is based on your character and integrity, which is all about what you do when no one is watching.

what I wish I'd known about:

power

Your man energy described at the beginning of this book has the potential to be an awesome resource for you. It can be fully used or it can be wasted. It's important to understand true power: who has it, who doesn't and what you can do to ensure others don't exert their power at your expense.

I used to keep chickens (before a fox killed them all one night). It was fascinating to observe their behaviour. Within all chicken flocks there's a pecking order. The more powerful chickens use their beaks to literally peck at the less powerful. It is cruel and painful for the victims. Among humans there is also a pecking order. You need to know how it works.

The next time you're among a group of people (including friends), look closely and see if you can figure out who has the most (or the least) power.

Powerful, influential people are great observers. They understand the subtleties of people, their strengths, weaknesses and insecurities. They recognise the dynamics within groups. They know who has influence, who thinks they have it and those who don't. And they quietly use their observations to exercise and enhance their own power.

Of course there is always the potential to misuse power to manipulate others. What sort of man you become will determine how you use power and influence. That's up to you.

These are just some of the factors that affect your ability to exert power and influence. Understanding this from an early age can be enormously beneficial to you professionally as well as personally.

The definitive book on understanding power and influence is *The 48 Laws of Power* by Robert Greene and Joost Elffers. Here are some of their findings:

Make the boss look good. Don't ever try to outshine him/her. Never let everyone know your intentions. Say less than you need to. Know more than you share with others. Take your reputation very seriously indeed. Develop it through your actions and the company you keep. Guard it. It's all you have. Be worth talking about (for positive reasons). Stand out. Draw people to you. Don't be known as someone who chases after others (that includes women). Avoid miserable or unhappy people. Devote more time with happy successful people. When you want help, realise that others respond better if there's something in it for them. Don't appeal to their mercy or gratitude. Know when to leave. People with the least power tend to stay to the end. Be unpredictable. Be very careful who you commit to. Never appear rushed. Always remain calm. Once you make a decision, be bold. Cultivate the appearance that your achievements were easy for you. No one needs to know how hard you work. Always appear less smart than you are.

If you have concluded that power isn't important to you – you'd better get used to not having any!

"When you don't have a plan, you become part of someone else's." Anonymous

what I wish I'd known about:

negotiating

No life skill has more potential to improve your personal power than an ability to negotiate: lower prices, better deals and more favourable terms. We all negotiate every day whether it's with family members, schoolmates or work colleagues. So it makes sense to understand how negotiating works.

When you know the process, you can become extremely skillful relatively quickly. And the benefits are not only immediate (for example, you pay less for the items you buy), they also help improve your reputation and success for the rest of your life. In short, you can seriously improve your life by knowing how to negotiate.

The skills you use as a good negotiator are useful in many other spheres of life too: confidence building, social skills, being more cooperative and reading people by gaining a more accurate understanding of the intentions and motivations of others.

First, let's dispel a myth about negotiating. It is **not** about being a ball-breaking tough guy who crushes his enemy by extracting every penny from a deal. That's win-lose negotiating: I win, you lose. It happens (and some will try it on you sometime) but it isn't that effective. Win-win: I win and so do you negotiations are far more preferable. Your ability to find a 'better way' is the mark of a skilled negotiator.

Negotiating can be extremely complex, but in this section we'll cover some of the basics about getting lower prices on the stuff you buy and how to persuade people to give you more of what you want, and be happy to do so.

I recently found myself needing a room at a hotel. I didn't have a reservation. I ended up paying just half what it should cost. Earlier this morning I called my insurance company to renew a policy. I was offered interest-free credit. Within two minutes I received a £60 discount.

Another time I was buying a sports car, and with some coaching by the UK TV presenter and motoring journalist Jason Dawe I ended up saving £3,500!

When the process was explained to me, it was miraculous to see how the negotiation unfolded.

My secret weapon was this: I just asked!

It is as simple as this: learn the following words and use them whenever you get the opportunity: *"What's the best price you can offer me?"* In so many cases this one sentence alone will either get you a lower price instantly, or it opens up a conversation which leads you towards a better deal.

Think of the quoted price simply as the MOST the seller ever expects to receive. All you have to do is find out the **least** they are prepared to accept.

what it takes to negotiate

Before you engage in negotiating there are a number of ideas it helps to be aware of. First and foremost: initially it takes courage. Don't be intimidated. Adopt the mindset that negotiating can be fun. Because it is. Even though everybody negotiates all the time, there's a widespread unspoken belief in the West that there's something a bit tacky about haggling. Put those thoughts out of your mind. Effective negotiations are conversations. Bad negotiations are usually arguments.

Good negotiators are always professional, calm, polite, friendly and respectful. Why? Because it always helps you get a better deal. No one wants to give concessions to people who are rude, angry and unreasonable. This is fundamental to effective negotiation. As your skill and confidence grows, you will gain far more respect and you'll get better outcomes.

This point is absolutely critical: know what you want! It's amazing how many people are prepared to negotiate but have no idea what their preferred outcome is. Think about it before you start negotiating. Ask yourself what you must have, what would be great to have, what you'd be prepared to settle for and what you refuse to accept. Where is the 'wiggle room'? What are the points you are prepared to discuss and what is not negotiable? But be flexible.

Know what the other person wants, too. By understanding the intentions and motivations of others, you can use that knowledge to get a better deal for yourself. Never decide or guess what they are prepared to accept – ask them. Then focus on the gap between what you each want and see if you can find a way to get what you want as well as allow them to get what they want. Sometimes this requires a bit of creative thinking. The objective is to work with them not against them. Work together to reach a solution that is good for both of you. Help them to feel good about negotiating with you. It doesn't have to be unpleasant.

If a company has genuinely let you down or given

you poor service, provide a detailed explanation of how they failed you. Pause. Let the other person speak. Don't interrupt. Pause again and then calmly ask, *"What are you prepared to offer me as compensation?"* Because you've thought about it ahead of time, politely tell them what you think would be fair.

All of this preparation can have a massive effect on the outcome of a negotiation. By thinking it through beforehand, you are less likely to have to think on your feet, which can be difficult.

Know when to shut up. After you've discussed the deal, make your considered offer. Then stop talking. Let the other person own the 'embarrassing silence'. This is what professional sales people do to potential customers. They know it gets a lot of people to say 'yes'. Be aware when it's being done to you!

Don't ever let the seller know how much you want something. It weakens your position.

Understanding your position in a negotiation is essential. For example, if you're buying the latest 'must-have' technology, your position is weak. The seller can afford not to negotiate. Whereas if someone is selling because they have a monthly sales target to reach and it's the last day of the month, your position is much stronger.

Before you ever buy an expensive item, it is essential that you do your research ahead of time. Search the Internet for prices, specifications and model numbers. Know what you're talking about. Print out the best deals. Take them with you. Make sure you're comparing like for like products. Printed materials carry far more weight in a negotiation than merely saying you've seen a better price 'somewhere'.

If you're dealing with a salesperson, printed

comparisons help them to find ways to justify giving you a better price or terms. They can't just give you whatever you ask for as they are often answerable to a sales manager and need to be able to give a logical reason why they gave you the deal. When buying a high priced item, professional negotiators often respond in this way: they suck in air, purse their lips, pause and say, *"That's a lot more than I was expecting."* This is acknowledged as part of the negotiation game! If a sales person ever asks you *"What price did you have in mind?"* this is a clear sign that he or she is open to a discussion and knows that he/she is dealing with a negotiator. Game on!

Know when to walk away. Don't ever let the seller know how much you want something. It weakens your position. And never allow your ego to keep 'fighting to win' when you also know that you don't want what's on offer that much.

You will eventually encounter unethical liars and cheats. Don't ever become one yourself. You really don't need to be when you know how to negotiate professionally. Maintaining your integrity will mean that people will trust you. Earn and deserve that trust. This has a massive effect on your long-term reputation. We'll cover how to identify when you're being manipulated or deceived a little later with some tips on how to handle those situations.

These are useful negotiation questions for you to ask:

- *"Is that the best price you can offer me?"*
- *"What do you need, for this deal to work?"*

- *"What's negotiable? What isn't negotiable?"*
- *"I really like it, but this is all the money I've got."*

Each time you get what you want in a negotiation, you improve the likelihood that you will get a better deal the next time too. It doesn't have to be at the expense of other people.

The best place you can practise your negotiating skills is probably a local car boot or yard sale. Among the junk you will find absolute bargains. Few sellers ever expect a buyer to accept their asking prices, which may be rock bottom anyway. Everything is therefore negotiable! You can practise at very low cost. Why not go along with some friends? Decide on the maximum you are each allowed to spend and agree to meet up again in, say, 30 minutes to show each other what bargains you've managed to nab. Split up. Don't hunt in a pack! And don't buy any stuff you don't want or need just because it was cheap!

Whatever savings you make from all your future negotiations, put the money you saved into your capital account as described in the money section. If you had paid full price for an item that money would have disappeared anyway – so put it to good use!

how to protect yourself
Paying lower prices is only part of what negotiating is about. Suppose you are asked to do something you don't want to do by a mate, girlfriend or family member. You don't have to go along with everything other people want all the time. Discuss alternatives

at least sometimes. Being an easy-going guy is admirable but you need to ensure that no one ever thinks of you as a 'pushover'. Occasionally asking for something in return is reasonable.

If you're ever asked to do something 'out of the blue', this could be a ploy that isn't as spontaneous as it might appear. It's often used by manipulative people to get their own way, at the expense of their 'victim'.

If you're ever put on the spot and don't know what to say about a request or an offer say, *"I'm open to your offer/idea. Tell me more about it before I make a decision."* This tells the person you're taking them seriously, but you are not prepared to commit to a decision too quickly. If you would prefer time to think about something further, say so. Don't allow yourself to get cornered into making decisions too soon.

Sometimes, you'll be set a time limit by the seller. If you feel pressured, simply walk away from the deal. If the seller then tries to reel you in, in a different way – beware!

In business, I'm often asked this question: *"Are you prepared to negotiate your fees?"* My answer is often, *"Yes. You can pay me more."* They usually laugh and agree to my fee.

Being seen to negotiate is a sign that you are self-confident and assertive. If your negotiating style is aggressive you'll appear arrogant. Even though it might feel thrilling to negotiate like a 'tough guy', you'll often end up with a worse deal.

There is no better way to flex your power muscles than by learning the art of negotiation. The sooner you begin, the more power you will start to attract. Negotiation is a fascinating topic. Study it to become a master.

what I wish I'd known about:

life skills

Certain skills are still 'expected' of men. Knowing how to do all of the following will make your life easier for yourself and demonstrate that you are capable of being independent. Therefore, find an expert who knows how to do each of these tasks well and ask to be taught each skill.

- Wire an electrical plug (safely!)
- Change and repair a bicycle wheel
- Change a car wheel
- Jump start a car
- Set rodent traps and dispose of any dead bodies
- Trap and dispose of spiders and wasps
- Repair a leaking tap by replacing a washer
- Mend a toilet cistern
- First aid: including mouth-to-mouth rescusitation
- Give a good non-sexual massage
- Iron your clothes (women especially are impressed by a man who knows how to iron)
- Know how to separate dirty laundry and use the different settings on a washing machine
- Sew on a button with needle and thread
- Use a handsaw and be able to cut in a straight line
- Learn to cook

Cooking is worthy of special attention. Not only is being able to cook a life skill, when it comes to impressing women, you will be seen as a culinary god with mystical powers. OK, that's overstretching it a bit.

STOP. Before you skip this section, read this true story. I had a guy doing some work on my house. He was 38, recently divorced and, with a bit of trepidation, he was re-entering the dating world again. Just before he left one Friday he came into the kitchen to see me cooking. It was a really simple Jamie Oliver recipe. I told him if he wanted to really impress women, and to stand out from the crowd, he needed to learn to cook. He wasn't convinced at all. He came back to work on the Monday and told me how he'd met a woman at the weekend and had mentioned the work he was doing for me and that I was a *"really good cook."* He went on to say, *"I couldn't believe what she said. She instantly wanted to know where you lived! You 'pulled'. And you hadn't even met her!"*

So, learn to cook real food. With proper ingredients. Avoid 'ready' meals. Putting a jacket potato into a microwave, or defrosting a pizza does not count! You'll eat less junk so it's healthier too.

There is something deeply attractive and sensuous to a woman about a man who is prepared to cook a 'real' meal for her. Invite a woman for supper and cook in front of her without any fuss. Learn four or five dishes well without the use of a recipe book. Don't make a big deal of it. Just do it.

A lot of men and women regard food merely as fuel. It can be far more than that. Any man who understands this will make a very positive impression on a woman.

what I wish I'd known about:

random stuff

- Realise that short cuts in life usually aren't.
- Being sarcastic and saying mean things may make you feel clever. It's not.
- Add an ICE (In Case of Emergency) number to your phone.
- Remember that curiosity and enthusiasm are the most valuable traits in a human being. And they are free!
- Fill your life with stuff that's more interesting than TV and video games.
- In the shower, self-examine your testicles for any abnormalities or swelling. Go to the doctor if you discover anything abnormal.
- Results are always more important than what you promise.
- How you deal with personal failures in life tells the world more about you than how you handle successes.
- Life is tough. It is not fair. And it's not personal.
- The world doesn't owe you a living – it was here first.
- Engage your brain before putting your mouth in motion.
- Don't ever bother trying to prove yourself as a man. Just be one.

some final words

With so much male bashing in the media it's sometimes difficult to know if the behaviour of the majority of men is being represented accurately or
not. Are most men really that violent, unreliable,
weak, irresponsible and arrogant? Or are there millions of hard-working and trustworthy men who
take their roles as friends, lovers, fathers, employers and employees particularly seriously?

Don't agree with everything you've read in this
book. Discuss the most relevant topics with your
family and friends. Especially with your father if
he is a part of your life. If you don't have a father,
ask the men you admire what they think about
what it is to be a man. Use the information as a
springboard for further knowledge on what it takes
to be a real man.

Revisit topics from this book. If you are a
teenager, you are growing at a very fast rate;
physically, intellectually and emotionally. What
you thought about a wide range of subjects is
probably very different now to what it was only
six months ago. What isn't particularly relevant
to you today may be incredibly relevant in just
a few months time. In fact, you will almost certainly discover that what you read again in the
future could feel as if it has somehow miraculously been inserted into this book. Certain sec-
tions may even appear brand new to you. That's

because you have changed so much in such a short time.

If you have found this book particularly helpful please tell your friends about it. And ask them to visit DearSonBook.com and the Dear Son Book groups on Facebook and LinkedIn.

Just be the man you want to be. Dress and behave exactly the way that suits your style and personality. This book has been a sincere attempt to guide you towards being the best version of who you choose to be as a man. Enjoy the journey.

The world needs a far higher proportion of responsible, real men.

You are invited to be one of them.

IF...

IF you can keep your head when all about you
Are losing theirs and blaming it on you,
If you can trust yourself when all men doubt you,
But make allowance for their doubting too;
If you can wait and not be tired by waiting,
Or being lied about, don't deal in lies,
Or being hated, don't give way to hating,
And yet don't look too good, nor talk too wise:
If you can dream - and not make dreams your master;
If you can think - and not make thoughts your aim;
If you can meet with Triumph and Disaster
And treat those two impostors just the same;
If you can bear to hear the truth you've spoken
Twisted by knaves to make a trap for fools,
Or watch the things you gave your life to, broken,
And stoop and build 'em up with worn-out tools:
If you can make one heap of all your winnings
And risk it on one turn of pitch-and-toss,
And lose, and start again at your beginnings
And never breathe a word about your loss;
If you can force your heart and nerve and sinew
To serve your turn long after they are gone,
And so hold on when there is nothing in you
Except the Will which says to them: 'Hold on!'
If you can talk with crowds and keep your virtue, '
Or walk with Kings - nor lose the common touch,
If neither foes nor loving friends can hurt you,
If all men count with you, but none too much;
If you can fill the unforgiving minute
With sixty seconds' worth of distance run,
Yours is the Earth and everything that's in it,
And - which is more - you'll be a Man, my son!

Rudyard Kipling (1865 – 1936)

thank you

So many men and women have contributed to this book. Thank you.

Special thanks to the following:
Vanessa Anderson, Geoff, Mark and Martin Bendle, Steph Bennett, Trish Bertram, Kurt Christopherson, Chrissie Godson, Sarah-Jane Hawkins, Chris and Elliot Kane, David McDonald, Penny and Hugo Mallitte, Antony Parselle, Toby Proctor, Joe Robertson, Glyn, Jay, Mike and Darren Sheppard, Peter Simonson, Paul and James P Whatmore, Tom Williams, Tracey Wright.

calling all mothers and fathers

What additional information do you wish you had known about when you were a teenager or young man or woman?

We'd love to hear from you so that the best insights can be included in future editions of this book. Email info@DearSonBook.com

We are also compiling Dear Daughter: what I wish I'd known at your age. If you have any insights to share for this book as a mother or as a father, please email DearDaughter@RoySpeaks.com

Thank you.

about the author

A former BBC reporter and news anchorman in London, England. Roy Sheppard is the author of numerous relationship books for business and personal. He is also well known for his work as a professional conference moderator for many of the world's largest and most successful organisations. As the 'conscience of the audience', he specialises in chairing complex, contentious and confidential discussions within an organisation. He is a visiting lecturer at Henley, one the UK's leading business schools.

He is an experienced keynote speaker on the subject of relationships, networking, reputation and referrals. And how to be upbeat in a downbeat world.

Visit www.RoySpeaks.com for more information.

charity donation

A percentage of the net profits from this book will be donated to Tools For Self-Reliance, a UK based charity supported by the author.

For 30 years, Tools For Self-Reliance has helped relieve poverty in Africa by supporting small businesses and by raising awareness in the UK. With the help of hundreds of dedicated volunteers in the UK, and partner organisations in Africa, Tools For Self-Reliance provides business skills and other training projects in six African countries. And each year the charity ships tens of thousands of refurbished tools and sewing machines to Africa and puts them into the hands of people who really need them. www.TFSR.org

other books by roy sheppard

How to Be The One. This book is about how to be a better boyfriend, girlfriend, husband or wife. www.BeTheOneBook.com for more information. The eBook version is called **How to be LOVED**

Meet, Greet & Prosper. Having hundreds of 'friends' you've never met on Facebook is one thing, but how do you start relationships? This pithy pocket book tells you all you need to know about turning strangers into friends.

Available as a **FREE** eBook. www.DearSonBook.com/MGP

That Bitch or **Venus: The Dark Side**. Co-written with Mary T Cleary, this book provides detailed information to help men and women protect themselves against these deeply disturbed, dangerous women who often prey on particularly kind, gentle men and women. These two titles are **exactly** the same book.

www.ThatBitchBook.com,
www.VenusTheDarkSide.com and
www.YouTube.com/TheDangerousWomen

Rapid Result Referrals. Practical ideas to generate more word-of-mouth and referral sales for your business.

All titles are available from your preferred bookseller or directly from the publisher at www.CentrePublishing.com